# ACCIDENTAL SUCCESS

Michael A. Dillard
MBA, MAcc

www.madillard.com

info@madillard.com



ISBN 978-1-7377828-0-3 print
ISBN 978-1-7377828-1-0 ebook

The views expressed in this document reflect the personal opinions of the author and are entirely the author's own. They do not necessarily reflect the opinions of the U.S. Agency for International Development (USAID) or the United States Government. USAID is not responsible for the accuracy of any information supplied herein.

*Thanks to Rudoh Dillard, my wonderful wife, for your selfless sacrifice and support. Thanks to my children, family and friends for your support and encouragement to write the book.*

# TABLE OF CONTENTS

# PART ONE
# ACCIDENTAL SUCCESS

# Introduction

The United States of America's total population is 330 million. The total number of US Diplomats is 15,000 or .004% of the entire United States population. Would you believe that a person who was raised in a single-family household by a mother who only earned a GED, who depended on food stamps as a child growing up, would go on to become a US Diplomat helping to eradicate extreme poverty throughout the world?

Well, this came to fruition for me in real life instead of it being a movie on the big screen. I would like to share my series of life stories to inspire hope in you and others who are contemplating a major life or career change.

Your big breakthrough in life is just a few steps away. You have come so far in your journey. Let's see the new version of yourself who is excited and waiting for you to cross the finish line. I know that despite how far the finish line may seem, you are closer than you think. I know this to be true, because I ran, jogged, walked, and then crawled across the finish line until I achieved my goals. Although the journey was hard at times, I refused to give up until I completed it.

In this book, I will personally share with you the secrets that I used to go from being unemployed on a Friday to becoming a US Diplomat on a Monday. If I had not been willing to fail forward, earn less today to earn more tomorrow, and implement a Vision Plan, I would not have been able to achieve numerous milestones outside of the United States of America that others dream of achieving in life. I have flown on a private 8-seater US Embassy plane, welcomed in person a former Secretary of State/Presidential candidate on her visit to the Dominican Republic, and learned from scratch to carry on basic conversations in both Spanish and French.

Once you finish reading this book, it will change the way that you think and live your life forever. You will learn to see obstacles as achievement markers in the journey of becoming the new YOU today.

What does a Diplomat do?

Before I tell you what a diplomat does, I am going to highlight the fact that I became a US Diplomat by accident. According to the Webster dictionary, an accident is an unforeseen and unplanned event or circumstance. As you read about my life stories, you will see why I call myself the Accidental Diplomat. Most people have heard of the Secretary of State referring to the great work that diplomats perform for the United States of America. However, who is a diplomat and what exactly do they do besides provide advice on prime-time CNN or FOX news about what is happening in a particular country? Well, here is your answer: a diplomat is someone who uses their personal relationships with officials and citizens of the host country to advocate for US interests, to work together on common causes, and to explain US society and values.

# My Broken Background

Both my mother and father dropped out of High School at an early age when my parents realized that they were expecting me—the most handsome baby boy in the world. They would later earn their GED, but that was the limit to which their academic peak was expected to rise for them during their generation. Thus, the standard for me was to get an actual High School Diploma, and then I would be deemed an academic success per my family's academic standards, ready to take on the world.

My memories of my childhood began with me living in Darmstadt, Germany, on a military base because my father was a supply clerk in the US Army. Living outside of the United States of America was a unique experience for me and my brother Tony.

We learned basic German phrases and indulged in German food such as french fries called Pommes frites and breaded chicken called schnitzels. On the weekend, the neighborhood kids and I would stop playing in the streets when the ice cream truck pulled onto our street. The ice cream was unlike any other ice cream. It was spaghetti-shaped ice cream swirled in your choice of chocolate, strawberry, or vanilla ice cream. On Sundays, the candy truck would pull up and we would buy coca cola shaped and flavored gummies.

When I was not playing in the streets with my friends, I was playing whatever team sport was in season at the time. I was the star running back during football season and, of course, the star point guard during the basketball season. At the grand age of seven, I was a standout athlete who was very talented.

Christmas at our house was like living in the actual toy store because we had all of the latest games and gadgets. We even had an Atari game console when it was first released. I was the man at playing the cartridge game super breakout and space invaders.

One day, my father came home and told us that he had received transfer orders to relocate to Ft. Campbell, Kentucky. Shortly thereafter, we were on a plane back to the United States of America. That summer, we spent time visiting my relatives in Norfolk and Portsmouth, Virginia. We eventually made our way to Ft. Campbell, Kentucky. We stayed in military temporary housing but had to move out because the place was infested with roaches.

We moved off base into a single wide trailer in Clarksville, Tennessee. My dad would drop my brother and me off at school on base and then we would walk to his work when school finished for the day. My mom and dad ended up buying a small three-bedroom starter home. The yard was so big that it took me three hours to mow both the front and back. It did not take me long to link up with the neighborhood kids and start playing basketball and baseball.

Since we no longer lived on the military base, we had to go to the public school zoned for our area. I was teased so bad for still having a Michael Jackson-sized afro when Krush Groove and the Fat Boys was blasting all over the radio, that I could not take it any longer and cut my hair. This is when my life took an abrupt turn.

My father and my mother separated all of sudden, which left my mom, my brother Tony, the newest addition to the family Darius, and I living in a house that she could not afford and without a car of her own to get around. My mother scrambled to get a job at a convenience gas station called The Pantry which barely covered the utility bills. It was a messed-up situation as I could not get free breakfast and lunch at school because my parents were still legally married. I went from being able to play team sports, having the latest pair of tennis shoes, and playing the newest video games to waiting on the 220 dollars' worth of food stamps to arrive in the mailbox. I recall very vividly the brown two-striped tennis shoes that my mother bought brand new straight out of the Dollar General Store. We started attending the Assembly of God Church on Ft. Campbell Blvd and a few church folks would give us some hand-me-downs every once in a while. I could no longer play team sports because my mom had to work, and she could not afford the registration fee plus uniform and travel costs. My life was getting sadder by the day.

I made it through the 7th grade by buying packs of Nerd candy and Now and Later candy for ten cents at the local convenience store and then reselling it for twenty-five cents at school. That summer, I signed up for a local youth job program, which placed adolescent youth in a summer youth work program. Bingo! Just what I needed. I was assigned to work as a janitor assistant at a middle school. I now had some change in my pocket to buy me a pair of real tennis shoes from the mall. I economized the rest of my money by buying my school clothes from Kmart. I could not wait for 8th grade to be over with so that I could get another summer job so that I could replace my worn-out school clothes. Once again, I was fortunate to get accepted to the Clarksville summer youth work program, which allowed me to earn some money so that I could buy some decent clothes for High School.

My freshman year at Northeast High School was a blast! I had come a long way from the time that I had returned to the United States sporting a tall Michael Jackson afro and black pleather outfit. I had become a fashion icon from the way that I remember it. I had a pair of brown eastland leather shoes that made every blue jean outfit hip. I would mix it up with a cowboy string bow tie. I was on another level with my outfits. And my hair was the showstopper. I was always putting an S Curl kit in my hair so that I could have the perfect baby curls. I would switch it up and buy the orange can of Murray's wave grease and put on a doo rag before going to bed so that the waves would be flowing by the time that I woke up and stepped on the school bus.

# Upward Bound

I was sitting in my 10th grade homeroom class at Northeast High School located in Clarksville, Tennessee, when my homeroom advisor told us about a government program called Upward Bound and handed us a brochure.

Upward Bound serves high school students from low-income families and high school students from families in which neither parent holds a bachelor's degree. The goal of Upward Bound is to increase the rate at which participants complete secondary education and enroll in and graduate from institutions of postsecondary education.

I had never heard of Upward Bound, so it was not even on my radar. Like a good student, I took the brochure home to my mom for her to read. Once my mom read the paperwork, she signed me up saying, "That it was something that would help me with my schoolwork." I was excited because the program offered a weekly $10 stipend which I planned to use to buy clothes.

So, what is Upward Bound? Upward Bound provides fundamental support to high school students in their preparation to attend college. The program provided in-person tutoring every Saturday on the campus of Austin Peay State University on Math, Science, and English, which are subjects that low-income students typically struggle with.

During the summer I attended an eight-week summer camp, which exposed me to world culture and art, in addition to the core Math, English, and Science courses. I recall going to the Tennessee State capital and seeing Goober the Deputy on the Andy Griffith Show eating lunch in the cafeteria. I also recall a classmate saying that he had returned from being in Will Smith's Summertime music video. We would listen to Humpty Hump, everybody do the Humpty Hump throughout the bus ride from Clarksville, TN, to Nashville, TN.

The weekly support came in handy because I relied heavily on the tutoring support to bring my grades up. Upward Bound changed the path in which my life was going. Exposure to seeing others succeed made it seem normal and achievable to me.

When I turned sixteen, I got a job at Ponderosa, which was a local American steak and buffet restaurant, picking up the dirty dishes on the tables, all thanks to a referral by a high school friend. Now that I was earning a steady $100 a week, I was on top of the world, since I could afford to buy whatever I wanted for lunch at the school cafeteria for the first time and buy clothes from the mall instead of Kmart.

When Ryan's Steak House opened down the street, Ponderosa started losing business. In order to put an end to serving a few customers throughout the week and the weekend, the owner decided to change the service. Instead of putting in an order at the counter and then sitting down to wait for your food to come to the table, it switched to having waiters and waitresses serve the customers at the table.

When I caught wind of the fact that they were training staff to become waitresses, I asked if I could become a waiter. I took to the training like a fly on a hamburger. I followed each of the six golden steps to serve the customer. I greeted every customer with a smile, took their drink order, returned to the table with their drinks, and was ready to take their order. I circled back to the table five minutes later to refill their drink.

When the bell rang from the kitchen window, letting everyone know that a meal was ready, I rushed to the window to grab my customer's food. I circled back two minutes later to see if their food was cooked to their liking. After about ten minutes, I would take some of the dirty plates off the table so that they could have room to let their bellies hang and give them one more refill for the road. The tips came in $2 to $3 at a time. Slow money is the best money because you can always count on it.

Little by little, I saved up enough money and bought a 1979 brown Chevy Impala for $1,000 cash. I called my car the Brown Hornet because it had a nice smooth caramel color. The car was made of pure American steel and two-inch windowpanes. It was all power and a true gas guzzler. Whenever I was at a red light, it would swing back and forth, waiting anxiously to show off its steel power of glory. Life was great.

As expected, my senior year in high school was coming to an end. I walked across the stage wearing my dark green Northeast High School gown, whose cap was laced with a gold tassel. In addition to my mom and brother, my grand dad, uncle, aunt, and cousin drove down from Virginia to watch me walk across the stage and receive my high school diploma. I had done it. I had broken through the GED ceiling. My mother and father were so excited that I had done something that they never did.

That summer, Upward Bound made everyone complete their Free Application for Federal Student Aid (FAFSA) and sign up for two college courses which the program paid for. To this day, I am clueless as to how I chose my major, but I decided to study Computer Science. I signed up for Speech and Introduction to Computer Science as my two free college courses.

Since I had been attending the Upward Bound Saturday sessions and summer camps, I was comfortable being on a college campus. However, when it came time to attend an actual college class with adults, I was nervous. I did not know how hard the classes were going to be, along with classroom etiquette.

The day had finally come, and I was off to my college classes. After attending classes for the first few days, I was shocked that no one was checking up on me or looking over my shoulders to make sure that I was studying and ready to take the weekly exams. It was every person for themselves to fail or succeed. While working forty hours a week, I went to class and spent the weekends with friends. The summer classes ended, and I passed my first two college courses. I was enjoying the college thing. I received an A in Computer Science and a B in Speech. Now came the real test. I signed up for five college classes for the fall semester while working a full-time job.

The first day of class was a blast. The campus was buzzing with all types of excitement in the air. The Seniors were ready to get the year over with so that they could graduate and the Sophomores, who had returned to college after their Freshman year, were ready to rekindle their old relationships and activities.

Although I was taking on a full load, in between class breaks, I would stop by the game room to watch an intense ping pong match. I tried my hand at playing ping pong, but I was no match for them. They would put all types of special spin on the ball when they served it to me, which would cause me to hit a high and slow return which they would smash.

The fraternities and sororities were out in full force, sporting their Greek letters. I attended a few of the weekly frat parties on the weekends whenever time allowed. Despite doing okay at the start of the semester, I struggled with Physics class because the professor carried out a lot of experiments which we were tested on the next time in class. Despite it being difficult, it was very informative. On one such occasion, I had fun doing the experiment of dropping a large ball and a small rock out of the window at the exact same time to see which object would land first.

To my surprise, my other classes were not too difficult. I was like: Wow, I can really do this college thing.

A friend of mine who decided not to go to college got a job working forty minutes away in Springfield, Kentucky, assembling stoves for

Frigidaire, making about $8 an hour. Since I wanted to earn more money, I applied to work on the 2nd shift with him, which started at 3:00 p.m. and ended at 11:30 p.m. After taking and passing a drug test, I was offered a job to work on line 4, assembling line drilling screws to secure the stovetops onto the stove's frame. I was ecstatic about getting the job because I was going to be making $320 a week guaranteed, plus health benefits.

After graduating from high school, my life was going so well. I was making great progress in my life and going to the computer lab every day because we did not have a computer in the house. I spent two hours a day working on and debugging my C++ projects, making tons of mistakes until the debugger returned showing zero errors in the 500 lines of computer code. To my surprise, I caught on to computer programming with ease.

Following a few hours in the lab, I would jump into the Brown Hornet and hurry home for a bite to eat before I hit the road for work. The Brown Hornet used up a lot of gas during my forty-minute commute to and from Springfield, TN, to

Clarksville, TN. I was having to fill up the gas tank three times a week, which was costing me a lot of money. I decided that it was time to sell the car and buy a car that used less gas.

Being the most intelligent person in my house as a young and dumb teenager, I went to the car dealer alone and bought a Program/Demo Car from the new car lot. A program car was a new car that the dealer used for errands, so it was slightly cheaper than buying an actual new car with zero miles.

The car salesman started off by showing me a few cars that were way out of my price range. When I informed him that I could not afford the cars that he was showing me, he walked me to the used cars and showed me a car that I had never heard of. It was a hatchback Geo Storm in electric blue. Young and dumb, I signed my name on the dotted line without even thinking about the interest rate that the bank was charging and how long it would take for me to pay the car loan off.

A few weeks later, I used my first student loan refund check money to tint my Geo Storm car windows and put shiny five-star rims on my car. I was not finished; I took it one step further and put 10-inch-wide chrome panels on each side of the car and had the words 2 Cool 2 Sweet engraved in blue letters on one side and Simply GQ on the other side with yellow neon lights underneath the car so that at night the undercarriage lit up the street as I cruised by. Oh, yeah! Life was good.

My life's ambition began to fade away once I started going to class at Austin Peay State University in the morning and driving to work in the evening every week.

I was spending eight hours a day on my feet in what I would describe as a large sauna. The moment that I walked onto the factory floor, the heat would smack me right in the face. The factory floor was lined up with four large assembly lines that made gas and electric stoves. Each line had about fifty people working on it. There was metal dust all on the floor left over from the metal residue that came off the screw as it was being screwed into the side of the stove panels by an air-powered industrial screwdriver. I would hear the large industrial fans blowing throughout the building in an attempt to try to cool the ninety-five-degree factory building. Almost everyone wore shorts and a t-shirt to not overheat.

As soon as the loud buzzer rang throughout the factory floor, calling an end to the shift, I searched for my timecard on the rack, punched out, and then made the forty-minute commute back to my mom's house. I was getting home from work at about 12:15 a.m. and then waking up at 8 a.m. to go to class again. In typical factory fashion, we would have to work overtime on Saturday whenever we did not make enough stoves for the week. The nonstop grind was wearing me out. Eventually, I just could not get out of bed to go to class.

I realized that I was at a crossroads. I had a choice to make:

Option 1: Make money Today working at the factory and drop out of college or

Option 2: Study Today and Make Money Later by quitting Frigidaire. I chose Option 3.

I decided to join the US Army so that I could make money Today, Study Today to learn an electronic trade/skill and get a college scholarship called the G.I. Bill which paid $36,000 for college.

*Become the new you today*
*and tomorrow, YOU will become*
*that person.*

## U.S. Army—Be All You Can Be! G.I. Bill And A Skill!

I saw the TV ads about being all that you can be serving your country while learning a skill and getting a scholarship for college. I strolled into the local recruiter's office and told him that I was interested in joining the U.S. Army, but I did not want to be in the middle of the woods sleeping in a tent during the freezing winter shivering my butt off for two to three weeks at a time like my father had to do in Germany.

The U.S. Army recruiter said that he had the perfect job for me but that I would have to score high on the Armed Services Vocational Aptitude Battery test that everyone has to take to determine what skills they have. He said that the job provided a sheltered van to work out of with a heater whenever I had to work for several weeks in the middle of the woods. Great, sign me up to become a Radio Repairer, I said to the recruiter.

I scored high on the ASVAB test to get the job and later passed the secret security clearance background check that I had no idea that I needed. In no time, I was told to pack a small bag and off I went to Fort Jackson in South Carolina for ten weeks of what is called Basic Training. During basic training you are taught how to act and become a U.S. Army soldier who is ready for combat.

By day two of basic training, I was singing Momma, Momma, can't you see what this world has done to me, Sound off 1, 2, Sound off 3, 4. Your left, your left, your left, right—left. This would be one of many songs that all new recruits would sing when marching in line under the direction of a drill sergeant. I had been too focused on the wonderful TV commercials highlighting the great fun, that I glossed over the fact that I would have to wake up early in the morning before the roosters crowed. After being able to sleep in every day till 8 a.m., 4:30 a.m. was way too early. What was I thinking? I learned first-hand that the U.S. Army really does more in the morning than most people do all day.

I was a whopping 128 lbs. when I joined the U.S. Army. Thanks to all the free eggs, toast, and bacon, I put on some weight so that the wind would stop blowing me from side to side. The U.S. Army really worked me into shape with all the running, pushups, and sit-ups that I had to do. I became a lean, mean, fighting machine in no time.

I had never held a gun/weapon in my entire life, and here I was toting an M16 machine gun built to destroy any and everything in sight. After a few days of training and practice with it, I became a pretty good shot at hitting targets up to 300 meters away.

At first, I was shooting twenty-six out of forty targets, then thirty out of forty targets and then thirty-six out of forty targets, which is considered an expert shooter.

Once basic training was over with, I went back to Clarksville, TN, to visit my family and pick up my one-of-a-kind hatchback Geo Storm before heading off to Fort Gordon in Augusta, GA, for eight months to learn how to become an Army Radio Repairer.

Life was a lot more chill and relaxed living in the government housing called the barracks, which held all new recruits that were learning their technical jobs. Every morning we had to exercise, march in line to go eat as a platoon of 200 soldiers, and then march to class. We would study for a few hours and then march to lunch, back to class to continue our studies, march to dinner, and then march back to the barracks. During the weekends we were free to do whatever we wanted as long as we were back in the barracks on Sunday by 8 p.m.

I was enjoying getting paid to learn a new technical skill that a lot of people paid thousands of dollars to acquire. I learned about the various components that were on most circuit boards like resistors, capacitors, and heat fans. I could read the voltage at various points along the circuit board to identify where there was a blown resistor or break along the circuit board.

After about five months in, I was able to use an oscillator to read the electrical current, use an ohmmeter, read schematics, and solder electronic components onto a circuit board.

Thirty-two weeks of training came to an end and I was ready to drive off to my first official U.S. Army assignment at Fort Carson, Colorado. Fort Carson was high up in the mountains. The altitude was so high that I had to catch my breath whenever I had to walk up a long flight of stairs. To my surprise, I was no longer the lean, mean, fighting machine that I thought that I was. The Colorado altitude got the best of me and I failed my first officially timed run. After doing some extra cardio, I was back on track to being a lean, mean, fighting machine.

The time had come, and our unit had to go to the field/woods to work and live for a few weeks. Since I was the lowest ranking member in my section, I was ordered to drive a 2½ ton truck packed with all of our equipment in the middle of the night with only a tiny glow light instead of headlights that shone no brighter than a glow stick. To me, this was just insane, but hey, if this was what was required of me to stay alive so that the enemy could not see me driving in the middle of the night, I would happily oblige. From this experience, I learned that it is amazing what you can achieve in life when you are forced to do it.

My assignment was up at Fort Carson, Colorado, after only serving there for twelve months. I guess the needs of the U.S. Army at that time required that my talent be sent to Camp Casey in South Korea.

When I finally arrived, I was shocked to see skinny cows grazing in large dirt fields with no grass in sight. The living arrangements were nothing to write home about either. I shared a room the size of most people's bedroom with two other people. I could not believe the living conditions. Now this was a real culture shock for me because this was not included in the U.S. Army recruitment videos. I was literally miles away from the United States for the first time as an adult, which brought about all types of personal feelings about life. I settled in and made the best of an interesting situation in which I had no control over. I could not get the image of skinny cows grazing in dirt out of my mind, so I stopped drinking milk.

The office was a ten-minute walk from the barracks and two minutes away from the cafeteria. There was nothing for me to do besides going to the gym to work out. There was not a kindle to read, a movie to watch on Netflix, or YouTube to binge out on since the Internet did not exist at that time. I was not a big drinker, so I did not drink down cases of beer until I crashed like some soldiers did to pass time on the weekend.

In order to stay sane, I would exit the base by foot and stroll across the street to pick out custom-made pajamas, hats, and leather jackets made by one of the vendors lined up outside of the military base. My roommate Specialist Roberts and I both crunched the numbers and realized that we could make more money working overtime at McDonald's than what we were making in the U.S. Army. We also realized that we would have the freedom to wake up at whatever time we wanted.

After twelve months of time served working in Camp Casey with only one trip back to the United States to visit family and friends, I was off to Fort Stewart in Hinesville, Georgia, to finish the last months of my four-year enlistment. Being back in the United States of America was a huge relief. I was free to go anywhere that I wanted and there were plenty of things to do. The work was great, but at this point in my life, I was ready to start using my G.I. Bill for college and put my electronic skills to the test in the civilian world.

# If They Can Do It! I Can Do It!

After serving four years in the U.S. Army, I received my discharge papers along with the G.I. Bill to help pay for my college tuition to study computer science at Austin Peay State University. I cherished the electronic skills that I had learned as a U.S. Army Radio Repairer, but my journey with the U.S. Army had come to an end.

I turned in my black leather military boots and uniform and drove back to Clarksville, TN, to visit family while I searched for a job. I uploaded my resume onto Monster and CareerBuilder hoping that a recruiter would find it and I also applied for all sorts of entry-level electronic technician jobs. I received a job offer at a company in Atlanta, Georgia, soldering motherboards, but the pay was not going to be enough to cover rent, my car payment, car insurance, gas, and utilities, so I declined the offer. At this time in my life, I was driving a semi-new Plymouth Breeze, which made me car rich but broke as a joke. Life taught me a very valuable lesson about buying a car and not reading the fine print. I, Michael Dillard, had bought a brand-new car that I thought was financed for five years, which turned out to be six years when I took time to read the contract a year after buying the car. SAY, What?? I was Young and Dumb with milk still dripping from behind my ears.

As I was searching for a job, I had read in my career transition packet that the U.S. Army gave me, that if you notified your employer that you were resigning to join the military that you could be rehired at a position that was equivalent or higher than the position that you had resigned from. This was music to my ears. I dialed the Frigidaire HR department, told them that I had just completed service in the U.S. Army and that I wanted my old position back. The person on the phone conducted her research and sent me my paperwork to come back as an assembly line worker on the morning shift, this time at the pay that I would have earned had I received all my raises. This was enough to cover all my bills living in Clarksville, TN, so I took the job offer.

My military benefits were already paying off, which I cherished. At the same time, this was a bummer and a big letdown because I felt like I was right back where I had started.

That Monday, I woke up early in the morning and made the all-so-familiar forty-minute commute from Clarksville, TN, to Springfield, TN. Along the way, I noticed that little had changed except for a few new gas stations and houses along the route. I pulled into the very familiar Frigidaire parking lot and made the same walk up the ramp and onto the buzzing factory floor. I walked up to assembly line 4 and asked the supervisor which station they wanted me to work at. As I looked around, I saw the same faces that I had seen four years ago. This scared me because I could see myself being in the exact same place years from then with a wife and children to support. However, I had BIG, BIG dreams and I knew that I wanted to use my knowledge and not my hands to make a living earning more money.

As I walked around the noisy factory floor during the lunch break, I noticed that a few people seated upstairs had nice cushy desk jobs. I said to myself, I want one of those nice cushy paper jobs where the people sit down instead of standing eight hours a day on their feet. It was at that moment that I told myself, IF THEY CAN DO IT, I CAN DO IT. One day, I too shall be seated up there under the nice cold breeze of an air conditioner.

One morning, I strolled onto the HOT factory floor and glanced at the job opening board and my eyes lit up. Frigidaire needed someone to work on the 2nd shift to maintain the testing equipment for the gas stoves. The position required a basic understanding of electricity, AC/DC voltage, and the use of an ohmmeter. I applied and received an invite to take a test on all the basic electronic stuff that I just so happened to have learned as a radio repairer. I passed the test and was offered the job to start the next Monday.

I met my supervisor in the main office and then he walked me to the office in which I would be working out of. The office was situated next to the cafeteria with no windows to see inside or out. He slid the door open, and a PUFF of cold air smacked me in the face. The A/C was cranked up to full ice-cold mode, which made the office nice and cold compared to the ninety-degree heat on the factory floor that morning. I DID IT, I told myself on the inside! I had a nice comfy chair and nicely air-conditioned office all to myself. While completing my college studies in order to become a well-paid manager, I kept saying to myself, IF THEY CAN DO IT, I CAN DO IT!

# FAVOR!

One Sunday morning at about 5 a.m., I heard a loud train sound coming from outside my studio apartment window, which was odd because I did not live near a train route. Then, all of a sudden, I heard a vociferous BOOM! I was like: What the HECK was that? I glanced outside the window and saw that the building straight ahead was on the GROUND! I then heard doors opening and closing as all the tenants quickly scrambled and ran down the steps to the underground basement for safety.

After about thirty minutes, someone went upstairs to assess the damage and to see if it was all clear. After hearing from them that the tornado was gone, I walked up the steps to see what had happened. I could not believe my eyes. The entire street was TORE up. The front windows of all the stores were busted out of their frames and glass was all over the streets.

Knowing that I was car rich and without a penny in my bank account to spare, I was very reluctant to see what my car looked like after seeing smashed up cars and other overturned cars along the street. Yep, my windows were cracked but since I had tinted window film on them, there was barely any damage on the inside of the car compared to the other cars that surrounded mine. The tinted window film had served as a blanket of protection. My car was sandwiched between a few others. The car had a lot of minor scratches and a few small dents, but it was drivable.

I walked around the block to get an up close visual of the damage all around. To my surprise, most of the buildings in the area had fallen or encountered significant structural damage. Later that day, we were informed that FEMA had set up an assistance office a few blocks away to help us find food and shelter. I caught a ride from a friend to the makeshift FEMA support center to search for my next meal and place to stay. I was officially homeless with nowhere to stay—for the first time in my life.

After waiting for a few hours to register with FEMA, I received a cash voucher for food and rent, which allowed me to continue with my life. The financial implication for my car was a totally different story since I had twenty-eight months of car payments left to make. The car had water-soaked seats, cracked windows, and some minor dents, and when I was allowed to get my valuables from out of it and drive it, I needed to check if it was actually drivable. I was relieved when I put the key in the ignition, and it started right on up. I put air in the tires and taped two clear plastic bags to create makeshift windows. I then drove the vehicle to the insurance adjuster and waited to learn how long it would take to get the car repaired.

Fortunately, the U.S. Army stressed that everyone had to always have car insurance in the event that we were involved in a car accident. They were so meticulous about this rule that they would conduct vehicle checks during every three- or four-day holiday weekend to make sure that our vehicles were roadworthy and insured. The landlord called me to let me know that I could come to the building between set times to gather my belongings. I parked a few blocks away from the apartment building and walked past piles of glass, metal, and damaged furniture until I reached the apartment building. The only reason it was still standing was that it was an old building made of thick steel as it used to be a hotel. I made several trips back and forth into my apartment until it was empty.

A few days later, I received a call from the adjustor from the auto insurance company. They informed me that the car was considered totaled. I was devastated because this meant that it would cost me more to fix the car than the car was actually worth at the time. I was told that the insurance company was going to send me a check for what they valued the car at and not the purchase price.

Days later, I got a nice $7,000 check in the mail and then I was like: Why does the check have the finance company name on it? Well, I was given another life lesson. Since the car was not paid for, I owed the bank their $5,000. I was forced to sign the check and hand it over to the bank who then sent me the difference. So, I ended up with about $2,000 to fix all the dents, buy new windows, and paint the car. I took the car to a local repair shop and they whipped the car back into shape.

After learning that I could get a BS degree in Music Business, I moved to Murfreesboro, TN. The music business classes were top-notch. The professors that taught the course actually worked or had contacts in the music business.

One of the professors used to manage Justin Timberlake, and another professor had written a must-read book about the music business. My college roommate and I started a music company from the living room of our dorm called CEO Entertainment, which featured two recording artists named Big Fella and Te'Arthur. They entered a Middle Tennessee State University recording competition for the chance to have a song recorded by Dave Aron, who was Snoop Dog's personal sound engineer. The duo won the contest and they recorded Hustlin' in Babylon right out of the MTSU recording studios.

After reading through all of the books in advance of taking the actual music business classes, I decided to change my major to an interdisciplinary degree so that I could become more competitive in the job market once I completed all the required college courses. There were some great moments for Big Fella and Te'Arthur, which included opening up for Kanye

West at the Nashville, Tennessee riverfront. Soon it was graduation time, and my family was buzzing with joy because my brother Tony was graduating from Austin Peay State University a day before me. Wow, my brother and I had come a long way.

*Your road to success will have lots of turns and hills, but as long as you keep taking small steps forward, you will reach your destiny in your time.*

# Earn Less Money Today To Earn More Money Tomorrow

My spirits were crushed because I had graduated from Middle Tennessee State University (MTSU), located in Murfreesboro, Tennessee, without landing a coveted dream job that would rain dollars upon dollars upon me so that I would no longer live paycheck to paycheck.

Since I had to pay for rent, utilities, and car insurance after I graduated from MTSU, I started working as a customer service representative at T-Mobile, hoping that I could apply for an assistant manager or manager-in-training position once I got my two feet in the door. Meanwhile, I kept scanning the MTSU career advertisement section to see if there were any newly advertised jobs for recent college graduates such as myself.

One day, I saw an advertisement for a paid eight-week internship at Union Planner's Bank. I decided to apply for the internship because I could not get a job as a personal banker. When I graduated from college, I applied to SunTrust Bank but was turned down because I had zero years of work experience. No experience = no job; no job = no experience. This was the terrible dilemma that I kept encountering, like a broken CD that kept repeating and repeating the same line in a song.

A few days after applying online for the internship at the bank, I got a call to come in for an interview, which I gladly accepted. However, to my dismay, I found out that the hourly pay for the banking internship was lower than what I was currently making at T-Mobile. Since I had zero years of that all so coveted professional banking experience, I told myself that sometimes in life you must value the experience that you will gain tomorrow more than the hourly pay that you receive today.

In total, there were about twenty of us who had been selected for the internship. For each tasker, I worked hard every day making sure that I marked my work with excellence so that I could stand out and get hired at the end of the internship. No matter how small the task was, I volunteered to do it. I would research old bank accounts that needed to be closed, pull transaction details from old files to close out a loan, and other random bank stuff. I did not want luck or chance to play a role in me getting hired once the internship was over. Although I had a foot in the doorway, I wanted a desk in the building.

As each day passed, I was acquiring more and more "banking" experience. I made myself an asset to the bank's staff. Well, the time had come, and the internship was finally coming to an end. My time with the bank as an intern was remarkable. If I had known the value of a college internship while I was in college, I would have made it my number one priority.

On the last day of the internship, I could not focus. I was extremely nervous about whether I was going to be offered a job at the bank or if I could actually get hired by another bank. My life was at a standstill because I had invested my entire future in gaining banking experience throughout the internship and I did not have a plan B. I was all in, folks.

Right before lunch, the banking staff thanked all of us interns for our great work and wished us good luck with our academic pursuits. They ordered pizza to commemorate the day.

After lunch, I was called into the office and offered a full-time position as a Mortgage Processor that paid more than what I used to make working at T-Mobile and the job included more benefits. I was amazed at how I was able to overcome the obstacle of no experience. Many people have graduated from college but are suffering financially, unable to get a good job because they lacked the required work experience to be hired. My Vision Plan was working. For the first time in my life, I felt like a legitimate college graduate with a fulfilling career ahead of me.

I saw a very nice looking and fit woman running on the treadmill one day in the exercise room at the apartment complex that I was living at. I greeted her and wondered who she was. I did what any guy would do and made sure that I came back to exercise at the exact same time every day until I ran into her again. Now, I would not call this stalking, I would call it checking up on the customer.

A few days had passed and there was no sight of her. So, I went to the gym in the morning instead of the evening since I had the day off. Oh, yeah, there she was, running like an Olympic sprinter on the treadmill. I had never seen anyone run that fast on a treadmill. I was ecstatic. I tried to play it cool, but I was all smiles when I passed by her. I hopped on the treadmill and punched in the same speed that she was going, since I figured that I was still Army fit. I was huffing and puffing after only two minutes; meanwhile, she had increased her speed. I was like: What the heck is going on here as I discreetly played it off as if I was doing a warmup before lifting weights.

Like a true gentleman, I caught her attention as she was leaving and asked her for her name, to which she replied, "Rudoh," and later her phone number, but unfortunately, she did not have a phone, folks! Now, I was perplexed by her response. I did not want to stalk her, but I needed to see her again so that I could get to know her.

The next time that I saw her at the gym we chatted, but she still did not have a phone so I could not get a chance to really find out who she was on the inside because she was all beauty on the outside. Hallelujah! The Lord is my witness.

One day, while she was sprinting on the treadmill, I heard a weird sound come from her direction. Ring! Ring! The ringing sound was heaven to my ears. Finally, I could call her to find out more about her. The Lord had answered my prayer. I began to envision myself having conversations with her outside of the gym.

In my gentleman's voice, I said to her, "If you don't mind, since I see that you have a phone now, let's chat later on."

She was like, "Sorry, but this is my friend's phone."

Okay, now people are babysitting other people's phones?

"Got it," I said. "Well, I am having a birthday party this weekend and you and your friend are welcome to come."

She said that she would come, but she was a No Show! I was devastated.

When I saw her at the gym, she said that something came up, but she really wanted to attend the party. So, I invited her to the movies which she agreed to since she did not have a "phone."

We settled on a day to make it happen. I picked her up and drove to Opry Mills mall to watch a movie. When we walked up to the cashier booth, she was like: I GOT it. I was like: Say What? You are offering to PAY for the movie tickets! Hmm, this is interesting.

Fortunately for me, the movie was great. On the way home, we stopped at the Mapco gas station so that I could get my favorite orange juice and pineapple drink.

She said, "I got it since it is still your birthday; it's my treat."

Well, at this point in my mind, I was like: This is a scene from a romantic movie. The night ended, and being the gentleman that I was, I offered to let her attend church with me at Mt. Zion Baptist Church. Fellas, the rest is history. Since that powerful Sunday morning sermon preached by Bishop Walker, we started to spend countless hours chatting on the PHONE.

# Career Change; Time For My MBA Degree

I was doing okay working as a Mortgage Deed processor for the bank, but my salary was not going to be enough for me to buy a nice big house enclosed by a white picket fence with a shiny red luxury car in the driveway. So, I thought to myself if I can get a Master's in Business Administration (MBA) then I can transition to a career in Management within the bank.

I decided to attend Strayer University's Nashville campus since they offered a flexible class schedule. The bank provided tuition assistance, so I took advantage of the wonderful benefit to help pay for my degree. As I was completing my MBA, I applied for jobs inside of the branch but received zero job interviews because I did not have experience managing people. Nevertheless, I kept my head up because I knew that one day I would be working in senior management. After I finished my MBA with a concentration in financial management, I received a few job offers to sell life insurance and stocks, but I was looking for a management job at the time, so I decided not to take any of the offers.

Later on, I applied and got a job at CitiFinancial. It paid more money, in addition to the prospect of working at Citi's corporate office. Things were looking promising for me.

Out of nowhere, I received an email from MTSU's career and development office about a job working for Dell Inc. in the Small and Medium Business Sales division, making $50K a year. Life Tip! You want to attend a college or University that has a top-notch career center which keeps in contact with its Alumni about jobs. This was the opportunity that I had been waiting for since I walked off MTSU's stage with my bachelor's degree in hand.

I filled out the online application and was called in for an interview. I passed the "sell me this pen" test and the behavioral interview with ease. With my start date set, I was ready to make some real money so that I could live the American Dream.

I was ready to put a ring on it, so I called Rudoh up on the phone and asked her to stop by my apartment for dinner. I cannot remember what we ate, but afterwards, on bended knee, I asked for her hand in marriage. She said, "YES."

As a small and medium business sales advisor, life was out of this world at Dell, Inc. We dressed however we wanted; no one cared if you had on flip-flops and shorts, or a suit and tie, as long as you got the job done. The last week of every three-month sales period, we would get free pizza, sandwiches, and snacks to keep us charged up to sell and finance more computers, servers, VMware, Logitech, Adobe software, and IT equipment. In addition to our 60% base salary plus 40% commission, there were all types of ways to make an extra $250, $500, or $1,000 a month.

With the money flowing in, I was ready to get married. Since Rudoh's family was still living in Zambia, we decided that we would have a small wedding reception in the United States and have a full wedding in Zambia, with all the bells and whistles.

While we were planning our wedding, I was winning all types of weekly sales contests and saving up for our big wedding in Zambia. If there was a team competition for who could sell the most McAfee anti-virus software, Dell printers, or Logitech accessories, I treated each contest as if it was my personal money to win or lose. Soon people on the team stopped trying to win, because I was HUNGRY for the money, and no one stood a chance against me. Once we had enough money saved up, we traveled to Lusaka, Zambia, to have a traditional Zambian wedding which would forever change my life.

Being newly married and back in America, life was great for us newlyweds. We were on top of the world. At Dell Inc., I wanted to be a Large Order Representative (LOR), so I updated my VISION PLAN and began preparing to apply for the job. You are probably wondering what an LOR does. An LOR works on large one-time $25K and above business orders. The job also paid more money, money, mon-eeey. As soon as a vacant LOR position became available, I applied. But I was turned down even though I had spent days practicing my responses to all types of interview questions. I was crushed for days.

When another LOR position became available, I applied again, and I was turned down once more. I was heartbroken. What would you do if this happened to you not once, but twice, for the same job? Would you give up, change employers, or apply for a different job instead? Well, I applied a third time, and the outcome did not surprise me. Upon hearing the results, I walked out of the room a BELIEVER. I was finally offered the job to be an LOR.

You must continue to trust and believe in yourself despite the obstacles that are in front of you. It will happen for you, as long as you refuse to give up. I got a promotion and Rudoh and I decided that it was time to buy a house since we were expecting our first child together. After about eight months, I was promoted to leasing and selling EMC servers, VMware, and IT equipment along with Adobe software to a dedicated account of 200 small and medium businesses.

# Unemployed With A Baby On The Way

After a few years with Dell Inc., I noticed that fewer and fewer people were ordering computers and that the prices kept getting cheaper and cheaper. This reminded me of the Beta/VHS era, which was later taken over by DVDs—this frightened me. I figured that it was only a matter of time before computers, like cassette players and VHS players, would become obsolete, so since I always had a passion for numbers, I started attending Liberty University Online to obtain a MS in Accounting.

Every weekend I would spend all day doing research for a project and writing papers. As I was finishing up my last few classes, I began applying for all types of US Government accountant jobs that were close to Zambia or on the continent of Africa so that we could be closer to Rudoh's family.

As soon as I graduated from Liberty University with a MS in Accounting in hand, the volume of sales across the computer industry began to decline rapidly due to the recession that was caused by the subprime mortgage housing crisis. The sales were so bad at Dell Inc. that I was eventually released while our second child was only months away from being born. Knowing that we could not sell our 2100 $ft^2$ house for what we owed the bank during the housing crisis, we decided to rent it out and move one block down the street into an 1100 $ft^2$ townhouse.

You must remember that in life, you will encounter setbacks, but it is how you handle the setbacks that will mold and shape your character. You only become stronger when you are able to take on more weight.

Thank goodness I had a MS in Financial Management from Strayer University, which taught me to be financially savvy enough to put money into my 401K account every pay period. In addition, I bought some Dell stock at a 15% discount every quarter through the employee purchase discount program. I was able to buy $1,000 worth of Dell stock for $850. A nice $150 profit every quarter plus or minus how much the stock increased or decreased in value. I cashed out my Dell stock, emptied out my 401K minus the IRS early withdrawal tax penalty, and applied for unemployment.

Since it was tax season, I volunteered at a local CPA firm filing individual taxes to add additional accounting experience onto my resume until I could land a full-time job with an accounting company.

After volunteering my services for a week, the owner decided to bring me on board temporarily until the tax season rush was over with, which was April 15th. During this time, I kept applying for all types of accounting jobs as well as a few management jobs, but the only job offers that I received were from Edward Jones to be a financial advisor, which I was passionate about since I love talking about retirement planning, or to be an assistant store manager at Buckle. Rudoh told me that no matter what we are going through now, I was not going to be knocking on doors for money or working long hours on holidays and weekends at a department store. She believed that God had something better for me and that my journey was not finished. She discouraged me from taking up the offer from Edward Jones and to continue searching around until a better opportunity presented itself.

However, we needed money in a hurry, so I decided to go to the interview with Buckle despite Rudoh's wishes. While I was being interviewed, Rudoh prayed against me getting the job even though we had another child on the way She believed that I was destined to do something better and bigger.

Five months before I had my interview with Buckle, I had received an email from an unknown company to go to DC to complete an in-person interview for a financial management job that I had applied for in October 2009.

When I researched the job qualifications and duties, I was shocked to find out that it required a medical examination, a lengthy background check to obtain top-secret security clearance, and that I was required to learn a foreign language. As I was doing more and more research about the job, I learned that the job was to be a United States

"DIPLOMAT" working as a Financial Management Officer overseas.

Up until the day that I was supposed to fly out for this interview, I kept practicing my answers for every type of behavioral question that they might ask me. I flew out of BNA airport and was picked up at the Ronald Reagan Airport in DC. I was driven to a nice corporate apartment that housed other applicants that were to be interviewed as well. They provided us with breakfast the next morning before being driven to downtown where the interviews would take place.

When I walked out of the interview, I knew deep down in my heart that I had passed. I just had a great spiritual awakening about it.

However, I had to wait for the results of my interview, which would be a few weeks depending on how many people they had to interview. When I returned to Antioch, Tennessee, I was so pumped about the thought that I could end up being a US Diplomat when I had applied for the job by mere accident, folks! But even though it was an accident, I needed it ASAP, because my wife's salary alone was not going to sustain us forever, nevertheless allow us to live the life that we dreamed of enjoying for the rest of our lives.

I was back at the local CPA firm hoping that after the tax season was over that I would be assigned to other accounting duties, but once April 15th came along, there was nothing for me to do. As I walked out of the office and closed the door, I was so sad. Tears started to roll down my face.

# Unemployed On Friday, U.S. Diplomat On Monday

A few weeks after my interview in DC, I received a conditional job offer to be a US Diplomat, but it required that I pass a medical and security clearance. The medical and security clearance can take six to twelve months before you find out if you passed or failed.

I was watching the news when there was a firm knock at the door and when I opened the door, there was a gentleman at the door holding a shiny FBI badge in my face. He said that he was looking for a Mr. Dillard. My heart began to pound loudly as I affirmed it and welcomed him into the townhouse. He said that he was there to conduct the interview portion of my top-secret security clearance for the diplomatic job that I had applied for.

The FBI investigator went through my job application and asked me questions about my personal life and work history. He asked if there had been any changes in my application and if I had a current job that was not listed.

"Yes," I said.

I informed him that I was UNEMPLOYED as he updated my file. He wrapped up by asking Rudoh, who was four months pregnant with our second child, a few questions and off he went to investigate my background. Since I was unemployed at the time, I was really, really, really praying on bended knee for this job to come to fruition as soon as humanly possible. I needed a J.O.B. like yesterday.

My friends, old neighbors, and former employers all received knocks at their doors by US Special Agents who inquired about my background. I was on pins and needles waiting and waiting for an email confirmation to come through stating that I had passed all the necessary medical and security checks.

The days turned into weeks, so I buckled down and decided that I would take the job at Buckle as an assistant store manager. Rudoh's prayer came through in typical fashion and two days after accepting the Buckle job, I was offered a job to be a US Diplomat with the United States Agency for International Development. FAVOR! USAID has about 1,850 diplomatic positions and most of them require that the person have a master's degree. And there you have it, folks, you can never go wrong investing in your education.

We were informed that we had to wear suits each and every day. I already owned two suits, so I bought three new suits from Kohls, along with a few ties and a pair of black dress shoes for my up-and-coming trip to DC, since they had a sale.

I started my training with USAID on June 10, 2010, to become a US Diplomat. During the training, they taught us about the history of US aid to foreign governments, the organizational structure in the United States, and the staffing structure of a USAID Mission in a foreign country. All throughout class, I kept thinking about Rudoh being in Antioch, TN, without me. Fortunately, her mother was visiting her while I was away.

I flew back to Antioch, TN, on July 3, 2010, and Joy was born on July 5, 2010. After holding Joy in my arms for a few days, I had to fly back to DC for flag day.

After weeks of orientation and learning how to fulfill the role of a US Diplomat, everyone is required to attend the last day of orientation in order to commemorate the training. This last day is better known as flag day and is one of the most important moments in a diplomat's life. It is on this day that everyone finds out where in the whole wide world they will be working for their first designated diplomatic assignment. The room is normally full of energy and the halls are buzzing with excitement. You can only imagine what it feels like to have your name called and then receive a flag for the country that you are assigned to.

The moderator officially welcomed Development Leadership Initiative (DLI) class 12 to flag day by saying that, "Today you will get a chance to find out which country you are going to start your first Diplomatic Assignment in." My Aunt Dr. Patricia Nixon, Uncle Jimmy Nixon, and my mom had driven up from Portsmouth, Virginia, to celebrate the completion of my 5-week diplomatic training and to find out where in the world I would be working. A few weeks back, I was asked where I wanted to go for my first assignment. Of course, I put Zambia as my first, second, and third choice.

I sat two rows from the front of the room and had a great view of all the flags that were sitting on the table that represented each country that someone would be assigned to. I searched the table for some flags of countries that I recognized but, to my disappointment, did not see the Zambian flag. Now my heart started to pound, and pound, and pound away as I realized that I was about to be assigned to work in a country that I had never visited and knew nothing about.

The Flag Day ceremony started with a few opening remarks and then the first flag was raised, and a name was called. Everyone clapped and congratulated the person that had just been called up. Then a red, white, and blue flag was raised, and my name was called. I was like, where on earth is this place? I graciously walked up to the podium, composed a fake smile for the camera, and then walked back to my seat, dazed.

As soon as I sat down in my chair, I heard a, "Wow! You hit the Jackpot!"

I am like, Huh?

The person seated beside me said, "You are going to the Dominican Republic. You are so lucky!"

I quickly dug into my pocket and googled the Dominican Republic. I could not have imagined what then pulled up when I hit the search button. Hundreds of beautiful beach pictures; all of them surrounded by crisp aqua blue water. I was like, Oh yeah, I can do this. After all the names were called, I scurried off to reunite with my relatives as people were congratulating and looking at my flag in awe and envy.

I had to call Rudoh to tell her the bad news. We were not going to the continent of Africa. We had mixed feelings about moving to a country where we knew no one. We were a little disappointed despite the beautiful beaches that we would soon be enjoying. The reason I had applied for the job in the first place was to work in Africa so that my wife and I could live closer to Zambia, have a chance to spend some time with her side of family, and get some additional help raising our children.

A lot of people in my USAID DLI 12 orientation class kept talking about buying groceries from Whole Foods. I had never heard of the store before, so two months after completing our training, I decided to visit the store before Rudoh and the girls arrived the following week.

As I entered the store, I could see how neat and organized everything was. At the entrance of a Whole Foods store you see all types of fruits and vegetables lined up. Being curious and not sure what to buy, I picked up a bundle of bananas and gently placed them into my basket.

I walked past the meat counter and noticed something that I had never noticed before. Whole Foods was selling grass-fed beef. It made me remember the old joke: What does a baby drink? How do you spell it? M.I.L.K. What do cows drink? Haha—gotcha. It only makes sense for cows to drink water and eat grass as they grow up to become big and strong.

I asked the butcher for a pound of grass-fed hamburger meat and was shocked at how expensive it was. I was like: This had better be some tasty meat at double the price of what I normally buy hamburger meat for.

After I checked out and made the stroll back to my apartment, I peeled open a nicely ripened yellow banana and bit into it. Hmm! Hmmm! This was yummy to my tummy. It was the tastiest banana that I had ever eaten. It was so full of flavor.

The following week Rudoh, and the girls moved to DC. When Rudoh saw the Whole Foods receipt in the drawer from the week before, she was shocked at how much money I had spent on so few items.

I told her, "Honey, you have got to taste the bananas, they are oh so good."

She was like, "Yeah right!"

I told her to hop in the car so that I could buy some more bananas, for her to taste them herself. In addition to the bananas, we picked up a few additional items. As soon as we walked out of the store, she bit into the banana and her facial expression changed from that of a skeptic to one of intrigue. I was right, the bananas were absolutely tasty, but was this just a mere coincidence? And what about that expensive grass-fed hamburger meat that I had paid double the price for, you ask? It was the BEST thing ever and worth every penny. The meat was so juicy and full of mouthwatering flavor. At that very moment, I started wondering what the heck had I been eating all these years.

Rudoh and I went back to Whole Foods the next day to do our weekly grocery shopping, but due to our limited finances, we bought salmon, hamburger meat, eggs, a few fruits and vegetables, and then drove down the street to buy our toiletries and household cleaning items at the other grocery store. Whenever we tried to eat non-GMO bananas and steroid-injected meat, the food tasted like fake food. We tried to save money by buying meat at different types of grocery stores, but we would have to drown our meat with all sorts of seasonings to get it to taste like something.

Surprisingly, after about a month of eating non-GMO food, I lost five pounds without doing any extra exercises and my energy level had increased. I guess what they say is true: you are what you eat because it is easier for your body to digest something that lives and dies.

Learning a new language to the point that you are expected to be able to talk about anything with other government officials in their native language was another level of learning that I had not anticipated. I thought that it was going to be just like learning basic vocabulary words in high school that I could just memorize at my leisure. Oh my, was I wrong. I had to be able to engage in a spur-of-the-moment conversation about the news, their life, where they are from, etc. I am not going to lie to you, it was very hard to learn a new language from scratch.

I would wake up at 7 a.m., eat breakfast, catch the metro, and arrive at class at 8 a.m. I would greet the teacher and the other students in Spanish to start the morning. The teacher spoke to us as if we were native Spanish speakers. We would often look at the professor in total confusion. Then one of us would say, "Por Favor Repitelo." Eventually, someone would catch what they said and tell us what we were supposed to do in the class.

From the moment that we entered the classroom, it was as if we were transported to Peru, Honduras, or the Dominican Republic because it was all Spanish in the classroom. English was not tolerated. We were being taught using an immersion language method, which is the only way that you can really learn a language. You must be in it to learn it. We would take a lunch break and head back to the classroom. Class would end at 2 p.m. and then I'd make my journey back home. I would spend a little bit of time with the family and then lock myself in the bedroom to complete my homework and review older material from past lessons. Every time we returned to class, we were expected to engage in longer and more detailed conversations. I would want to tell everyone about the great weekend that I had, but I often lacked the vocabulary to describe who, what, when, and where in enough detail that they could understand. So, I would just say that we went for a walk, watched a particular movie, and called some friends.

*You will achieve it in due time.*

It is true that some people appear to be better at some things, but do not let that discourage you because you did not see the work that they were putting in while you were watching TV, traveling, or working late.

I learned this the hard way when I became a US Diplomat and was assigned to learn Spanish at the Foreign Service Institute, since the official language in the Dominican Republic is Spanish. I was required to study Spanish for twenty-four weeks so that I would be able to communicate with the Dominican government officials and locals in their first/native language.

I received an email a few days before I was supposed to take my Spanish lessons, that included basic information about the course and my class schedule. I walked through the halls and located my class and took a seat. Soon, the class was filled with the other students. Eventually, the teacher walked in and greeted us all in Spanish. When the teacher kept speaking to us in Spanish, I was like umm can we slow this down a little bit. Then the teacher switched to English and asked us about our Spanish language backgrounds. I proudly told the teacher that I had taken High

School Spanish for two years. The teacher told us about her background, went over some basic phrases, and then gave us homework to be completed the next day.

After six weeks of going to class learning some Spanish grammar rules and vocabulary, I had to take a test to gauge if I was on track to pass my Spanish speaking and reading exam by the 24-week time mark. I failed the first 6-week assessment, which meant that I was not progressing as fast as I should have, which caught me off guard because I thought that I was doing an amazing job.

Up to that point, I had been spending ten hours a day for six days a week, reviewing my Spanish notes, and listening to the news in Spanish etc.

When I took the second assessment, it was official; I was behind where I should have been at the 18-week mark. Two days after being told that I was very behind, I got called into the office and advised that I was being sent off to a one-on-one language training facility so that I could catch up. I was devastated and morally defeated. In order to achieve something, you must accept the fact that you will fail at first. I had no idea that they wanted me to speak Spanish at a level in which I would have to give a full speech or conduct an impromptu interview with a foreign minister all in Spanish without making lots of grammatical or gender mistakes.

One day, I was on the DC metro going to my one-on-one Spanish class, and I thought to myself: How come these other people are so ahead of me and they all started class at the exact same time as me? Well, well, well: after talking to a colleague, I discovered that most of the people in my earlier classes had learned Spanish in the Peace Corp from living in a Spanish-speaking country, had studied Spanish for four years in high school and in college, or had a Spanish-speaking spouse at home to practice with all hours of the day. So, here I was comparing myself to everyone else who had a 6-year head start in studying the language.

You must remember that everyone comes from a different background and has learned different sets of skills because of that. You must not be intimidated by how well others are performing at something, just remember that they have a 6-year head start on you today but in due time, you too will also cross the finish line and achieve the same thing that they achieved.

At this point in time, I realized that in order to pass, I had to put in about ten to twelve hours of study time seven days a week since I did not have a background in the language. Like a revolving door, I came home from class, chatted with the family, and then did my homework and reviewed the previous materials that I learned weeks ago; every day for thirty weeks until I eventually passed.

In life, whenever you fail at something, try it again and again and again and so that you can become better than you were the day before. Although you did not reach your goal of losing ten lbs. in exactly one month, you did learn what works and what does not work until you lost that ten lbs. Failing forward is how people become a better version of who they were the day before.

After taking a foreign language at the Foreign Service Institute for the first time, most diplomats vow NEVER to go back there again because they are extremely meticulous and strict. The learning pace is very hard and fast at first with very little downtime. Spanish was so rough for me at one point that my wife told everyone that she had lost me to "Spanish" when I was learning the language.

I surely failed forward. In about thirty weeks, I went from not being able to say Hi in Spanish to being able to give a speech in front of several people. It is amazing what a person can accomplish if they are willing to make small, incremental improvements over a long period of time. After spending a brutal amount of time at the Foreign Service Institute to learn how to speak and read in Spanish, the family and I were Hasta Luego to Santo Domingo, Dominican Republic.

# The Diplomatic Life

After the movers packed up our belongings to be shipped to Santo Domingo, I was anxious to get to the USAID Mission in the Dominican Republic so that I could enjoy the fruits of being a US Diplomat. With our visas stamped in our diplomatic passports, we were ready to test out our diplomatic immunity. Just kidding!

We boarded the plane in DC, and within hours we were debarking the plane in HOT! Santo Domingo, Dominican Republic. As we made our way into the airport, I was reading the signs indicating where to go. I saw a sign that read DIPLOMATICOS and walked up to the counter. I greeted the immigration and customs officer in SPANISH, telling her my name, who I worked for, and what my job was. After addressing all her questions, we exited immigration and walked to the baggage carousel to pick up our suitcases. With our suitcases loaded on the trolleys, we walked to the arrivals section and looked for a sign with our name on it. Our sponsor had arranged everything for us. The SUV with a diplomatic license plate pulled up, and the driver got out and helped us load all our suitcases in the back.

The drive from the airport was magnificent. I saw the old colonial buildings that had been built years ago, tucked between new twelve-story high-rise condos. The view of the ocean was breathtaking. The crystal clear, aqua blue waves crashing up against the rocks were stunning.

Thirty minutes later, we pulled up to an eight-story condo that overlooked the city. Our sponsor explained to us that we would be in the condo temporarily until our standalone house was ready. The three-bedroom condo was fully furnished and had a great view of the city. Our sponsor really took care of us and had stocked the fridge with some basic food items to carry us over for the day. We sat on the balcony and watched the sun set, marking the end to a marvelous day.

The next day, our sponsor took us to a local restaurant in the neighborhood and then grocery shopping. That Monday, I put on my nice Kohls suit, ate breakfast, and waited for the driver to pick me up for work. After a week off in briefs, I was ready to start working. I was given a small office across from the bathroom and next to a conference room. I enjoyed the location of my office because I got the chance to talk to someone new every day. I was put in charge of approving payments for the Mission staff who had traveled for training or out of the city to monitor one of USAID/Dominican Republic's development projects, the utilities for the office, and funding for several of our projects. Each day, I was learning more and more about my job and the great work that USAID performs on behalf of the American taxpayers.

My life outside of work was more than I could have dreamed of. It was like I was in a family sitcom, which showed the world the value of having a vision, making a change, and then becoming successful. The traffic in Santo Domingo was too much for us to navigate, so when our car arrived from the US, we hired a driver so that he could drive me to work, drop our daughter off at school, and take Rudoh grocery shopping. We hired a housekeeper to iron our clothes and to do some basic house cleaning around the house.

We were the typical American family living in the Dominican Republic, enjoying food prepared by chefs and visiting the beaches, surrounded by aqua blue water. When we went out to 5-star restaurants—by American standards—we had our children with us, while the Dominicans left their children at home with the nanny so that they could enjoy life to the fullest. Not one of the many restaurants that we dined at disappointed us. The Pepper Steak on the Malecon: estaba Muy Rica! The local hand-chopped Chicharron stand down the side road: estaba Muy Rica! The Boca Chica fish: estaba Muy Rica! Toda estaba Muy Rica!

Everywhere we went, Rudoh and I had to communicate in Spanish, which caught us off guard, however, we quickly perfected our basic Spanish phrases and blended right in. We learned how to get directions to the various malls, find the best clothing shops, and order our favorite local Dominican dishes.

Working as a US Diplomat was great. I was so full of American pride and joy walking in and out of the building every day knowing that I was representing the United States Government. The local employees working at USAID were extremely professional and knowledgeable. Since it was my first assignment, it was technically a training assignment and thus my supervisor and the local staff were responsible for teaching me everything. Everyone working in the office was just so amazing. They taught me so much about international development, along with my financial management job responsibilities.

I would go to a meeting and I would hear them talking about a project's pipeline and I would be like what on earth is a pipeline? After every meeting, I would go back to my desk and search the new terms that I heard so that I could have a better understanding whenever the topic came up again at the next meeting. I was reading through my inbox of emails when I came across a USAID agency notice that was sent out to everyone about a new training program that they were piloting. This new training was being developed to train USAID employees on how to work with and conduct a financial assessment of a government entity. I eagerly signed up for the pilot training in

DC so that I could learn how to implement a development project through a host country government's financial management system instead of using the traditional method of hiring an implementing partner to manage the malaria, HIV, education, or water and sanitation project on behalf of USAID.

A few weeks later, after completing the training, my boss put me in charge of completing an assessment of the Government of the Dominican Republic's financial management system. This was such an honor. Who could have imagined that a person who once lived on food stamps, whose parents had GEDs, would be in charge of such an important political assignment?

Working with employees whose culture is different from yours and their government's officials requires emotional intelligence—so that you do not accidentally offend people. The success of the assessment depended on me not leaving anything to chance. I scheduled the days that the other USAID Diplomats and local employees would go to the various government ministries to interview the Dominican Government officials.

The level of responsibility was so overwhelming that I did not have time to think and reflect in the moment on exactly what I was accomplishing. I, Michael Dillard, was leading an assessment on behalf of the citizens of the United States Government. I was sitting in and organizing to meet with various Dominican ministers who had twenty to thirty years of government experience, and here I was, only eighteen months removed from being UNEMPLOYED, folks.

With the help of my Mission colleagues, the assessment of the Dominican government's financial management system was finalized and sent off to the USAID headquarters in Washington, DC. I appreciated the fact that my boss exposed me to all aspects of the job and did not hide me in the corner.

## You Are A Custom-Made Suit

Your journey in life will be different from everyone else's.

I remember going to the store and buying three suits from Kohls so that I could attend the five weeks of diplomatic training. I saw a nice navy-blue suit, but it was out of my price range, so I walked around several suit racks searching for an affordable suit that looked decent. I found a nice tan suit and went into the dressing room to try it on, but the pants were way too long and the sleeves on the suit jacket were too long as well. I walked back onto the floor and tried on some additional suits and then finally settled for three suit separates. The suits were just what I needed.

A year later, I was in Bangkok, Thailand, for training. I heard that you could have a custom-made suit created for about the price that it would cost for a good suit in the United States. I did my research and settled on a traditional navy-blue suit and a charcoal gray suit. I did the initial fitting and then came back the next day for the shell fitting and then picked up my suits four days later.

"Amazing!" I shouted.

The suits fitted perfectly on me. The pant length was just right, the suit sleeve was just right. The suit fit me like a glove.

When I walked into the office, people were like, "Wow! You look amazing! That suit really fits you."

My path in life will be different. Your path in life will be different. I may meet up with you at the mall and then afterwards you will drive home. I will also go home, which will be in a totally different direction. The way that you think, feel, and act is different and will be different because you are a custom fit and not an off-the-rack mass-produced suit. Embrace being different; enjoy being you.

# Apples And Oranges

Have you ever wanted to talk to a colleague about something that you needed to resolve and after the meeting was over and you are seated back at your desk, you realize that you still did not resolve your main issue? You were talking about apples and your colleague was talking about oranges.

Just recently, we flew to the United States for a long-deserved Christmas vacation. We wanted a house with an indoor fireplace so that we could roast marshmallows on the open fire. Well, when we arrived at the house, the fireplace was outside and not inside as advertised on Airbnb. To make matters worse, it was a gas fireplace, and it would not turn on no matter how long we pushed the different buttons down. We contacted the owner and they informed us that the fireplace worked just fine and that they never advertised the property as having an indoor fireplace. We asked for a deduction since the fireplace did not work and was not inside as requested. Our whole

Christmas tradition of roasting marshmallows each year had been ruined.

When we checked out, we filed a complaint stating that the property was not properly advertised. The property owner told us that after we had checked out, they had checked the outdoor fireplace and that it was working and thus they would not give us a partial refund. We politely told them that the issue was actually the fact that we checked the Airbnb amenity box for an indoor fireplace so that we would not have to be outside in 18-degree weather with the ice-cold wind hitting us in the face.

Then the property owner said that Airbnb had made a mistake by advertising the property as having an indoor fireplace instead of an outdoor fireplace and that we must ask Airbnb to pay us for the price difference. I kept the conversation focused on the indoor fireplace—the apple—instead of focusing on the outdoor fireplace—which was an orange. I must admit, Airbnb took care of us and provided us with a partial refund since the property was not advertised correctly.

Another example of how the apple and orange conversation can go is when you are talking with your spouse about why they did not do the laundry and then your spouse says to you that you never wash the dishes. You counter by saying to your spouse that you were just about to do the dishes. Then your spouse says to you to make sure that the dishes are dry before you put them in the cabinet. But if you recall, the purpose of the conversation was to talk about the laundry ☺.

As a Financial Controller, I am responsible for making sure that everyone adheres to the accounting policies and procedures of the USG. Sometimes people want to do something that is logical to them but just is not allowed under the current USG regulations. Having to go back and forth with someone about something that is so near and dear to them can become very emotional at times because the stakes are high for them.

I have a secret that I would like to share with you that you can use when you must have a difficult conversation with someone that works every time. The secret is to keep your eyes focused on the Big Apple and not to get distracted by the many things that have nothing to do with the issue. These are the oranges that people add to the conversation.

For example, what if Mark and I are talking about conducting a Risk Assessment of the Government of Tommy Island and Mark wants the project to be implemented in three weeks, but the typical Risk Assessment takes six weeks to complete, and then Mark starts complaining that I am taking too long to do the work and that it took two months for my office to approve his recent travel voucher. I would politely put the Big Apple back on the table and explain to Mark that the Risk Assessment takes six weeks because we must interview the Minister of Finance, interview the procurement staff, and interview the Department of Treasury, review their policy manuals as needed, and complete spot checks to make sure that what is listed in the policy manual is what is being done.

At this point in the conversation, the person has full understanding as to why it takes six weeks to complete the Risk Assessment and that it is not me personally who is holding things up. Upon finalizing the conversation about the Risk Assessment course, you are now ready to have a discussion about why the orange/travel voucher took two months to process. You should not eat the poisonous orange when you came to talk about the Big Apple. The next time that you are talking with someone and then they start to change the purpose of the conversation to something else or make the issue about something different, remember to keep the topic on the Big Apple.

*You cannot let your old self interfere with the NEW you. You need to always be confident in your abilities because just like them, you deserve to have a seat at the table. You earned it!*

After two wonderful years in Santo Domingo, it was time for me to bid/apply for my next job at another USAID Mission around the world. Since Zambia—which is known for Victoria Falls, one of the seven wonders of the world—was on the list, I was ecstatic about the thought of working in the country that was responsible for me becoming an accidental diplomat.

I interviewed for the upcoming Deputy Controller position in Zambia but was told that I was not their number #1 choice. I was shocked and surprised at what I was being told because I could not think of another newly hired person that had more financial management experience than I for what seemed to be a position for a junior officer.

USAID/Dominican Republic is a regional Mission with financial management responsibilities for Barbados, part of Haiti, Guyana, Jamaica, and Trinidad and Tobago.

I willingly took on the lead role for completing an assessment of a government-approved payments program for the region, and managed internal controls for the region's financial operations, which were higher levels of responsibilities compared to what my peers were responsible for working on. Even though they told me that they were going to select someone else as their number one candidate, I listed USAID/Zambia as number one on MY list of places where Michael and Rudoh Dillard wanted to work and live, along with a few other countries that I was okay with going to work.

As we nervously waited for the assignment list to come out, Rudoh kept telling everyone that we were going to Zambia and I was like, hold your horses in the barn, it is not looking good for us despite our VISION PLAN of being in Zambia.

Rudoh said, "I hear you, but we are going to Zambia because I have faith in God."

Let the church say Amen!

The assignment list always comes out in mid-December, which usually makes for a gloomy or happy Christmas for bidders. A few hours before the assignment list was supposed to be released, my work phone started beeping. I did not know what all the beeping was about, so I wondered what new international incident just hit the world news. When I unlocked my phone and clicked on the email icon, I saw a flood of emails pouring in, but I could not make out what the fuss was all about.

CONGRATULATIONS on your assignment, was on the subject line, but where, I kept wondering? I eagerly clicked on the assignments page and saw Michael Dillard assigned as Deputy Controller to Zambia. Wow, Wow, Wow, Rudoh's FAVOR was all upon us! Since we were moving to Zambia, we decided to have another child. We hoped that our last child would be a boy.

*In life, you must remember to point your boat in the direction that you want it to sail, and let God handle the rest. If you can Believe IT, you can Achieve IT!*

Once again, our household items were packed up and we were off to Zambia.

We arrived in Zambia on a Saturday to a caravan of friends and family waiting at the airport to greet us. I rode in the Diplomatic SUV per protocol, while Rudoh and the kids rode with her family members to the temporary house since our house was not ready for us to move into just yet.

Sitting in church that Sunday, I reflected on how my post-college career changed all because I wanted to talk to the woman who did not have a phone. It was all so surreal. I also reflected on the moment in time when I saw my beautiful wife walk down the aisle in this exact church. Our wedding day was an emotional moment for me. When I saw the beauty of my life in her beautiful beaded wedding dress, my eyes began to water.

In typical diplomatic fashion, on Monday a driver picked me up from the house and off to work I went. After a few days of getting to know the people, and the major development projects that the Mission supported, it was business as usual since the financial regulations are the same at every Mission.

A few months later, Michael Junior was born, which solidified our journey in life coming full circle. We had gone from barely having help when our first child was born, to having an endless line of people who were willing to change diapers, babysit, and look after our children for us. Every day, life in Zambia was yet another episode from a sitcom for me. Something that I could not have ever dreamed of or imagined. On many occasions, I would accompany my wife to the local market, an old friend's house, or to the loss of life memorials at people's homes. Individuals would be shocked to see me, the American Diplomat, at these memorials because of my work title. I would greet the women in the house and take a seat outdoors next to the rest of the men mourning the loss of their friend or relative. The people would try to roll out the red carpet for me by attempting to give me the best chair to sit in, put me inside under the air conditioner, or prepare a special meal, but I would insist that I was fine and that they must not go out of their way just for me.

I would say, "You all are so kind, let's just enjoy each other's fellowship and company."

Workwise, things started off very, very slowly for me with very little overall responsibility that would be worth getting promoted over. Rudoh and I convened a VISION PLAN meeting. We discussed the pros and cons of how our life would unfold if we stayed in Zambia for two years instead of four years.

We eventually decided that from a work/life balance perspective that life would continue to be amazing, but that I would start to feel as if I was trapped in a room without any doors. There was no way that I was going to be able to put together a portfolio of great accomplishments for the promotion board to deem worthy of a promotion. The VISION PLAN was updated.

I decided to leave Zambia and go work in Afghanistan for one year and then apply for an Office Director position at my next post so that I could get promoted faster. People were like: Are you CRAZY! Why would you and your wife leave after only two years and go off to Afghanistan, a war-torn country, of all places? These people did not understand the power of a VISION PLAN.

Once again, the movers were at our house packing up all of our belongings, but this time the family was moving back to the house in Antioch, TN, that we had been renting out.

As I reflect on our decision, it was the right thing to do, because a large number of people that I started with have not been promoted for years.

## The Secret To Kicking The Fear Out Of Public Speaking

In Zambia, I kept hearing a lot about Toastmasters and how they can make you a better speaker. Whenever time permitted, I joined a few sessions to listen to some of the speakers and to get an understanding of what the program was all about. I know that a lot of people are afraid of speaking in public because of the fear of making a mistake in front of others. Some of the top common reasons for the fear of speaking in public are self-doubt, making a mistake, and appearing nervous.

If you are like most people who have taken any type of leadership class, they make you take the Myers Brigg personality test so that you can know more about the reasons behind why you make decisions. Having taken many personality tests, they show that I am an INSJ. The I stands for Introvert. An introvert is a person that likes to keep to themselves and not be all out in public in front of a lot of people. So, the thought of speaking in front of people used to flood my brain with all types of bad things that would and could go wrong as soon as I opened my mouth. Yep, just like everyone else, I feared that I would flop in front of everyone, and they would laugh at me. I feared that the crowd would not be able to understand my accent. I feared that someone would ask me a question that I did not know the answer to etc.

However, my job as a US Diplomat required that I speak and talk to people in public at various receptions, meetings, and conferences. In order to kick the fear out of speaking publicly ASAP, I started doing what the other great speakers do and relied on a speaking format.

Here are the secrets that I learned from them that I want to share with you.

1. They learn a format.
2. They practice their format
3. They deliver their speech and then tweak it to make it just a little bit better.

You can use a Past, Present, Future format (PPF); Pros, Cons, and your Opinion (PCO); Advantages, Disadvantages, and your Opinion (ADO); Opinion about X, Reason for your opinion,

Example to support your opinion, and conclude with your Opinion (OREO). So, if you are at a reception and someone asks you to speak, you can use the PPF format to give the best speech ever. EXAMPLE: When I met Thomas in college, he was a person that knew everything about everything. We used to go to study hall together every Tuesday because the History professor liked to give pop quizzes at the beginning of class, so studying was a must. Ever since that day, we have been best of friends. Currently, Thomas and I lead Youth Bible Study together. I wish Thomas and his bride all the best in the future. I know that Thomas will make a great husband and that you both will live happily ever after together.

Now, if during a meeting, your boss asks your opinion about something, you can use the ADO to start off talking about the advantages of buying a brand-new building, then the disadvantages of buying a brand-new building, and then provide your opinion about what action the company should take. As of today, you are now ready to speak in public. You should pick a random topic and use one of the above formats to talk about the topic. You should make it a habit that during your next car ride, shower, or walk, you choose a random topic and then use one of the above formats to talk about it.

You must be willing to take the path that is meant for you and not worry about the paths that others choose to take. Yes, you will be criticized for not conforming to the status quo. However, you are uniquely made and therefore destined to take the hidden path that only your eyes can see.

Dubai Gold Bazaar

Soon the family was back in Tennessee, and I was working in Afghanistan. I lived and worked on a compound surrounded by armed military forces from all over the world. The place was heavily fortified and had hundreds of soldiers guarding the premises.

We were well taken care of since we could not go off the compound. We had waffles, freshly squeezed juice for breakfast, and all the chicken and beef that you can imagine for lunch and dinner. There was a 24/7 gym and laundry facilities scattered throughout the compound. My room was the equivalent of living in the back of a well-put-together semi-trailer. When you entered, there was a small desk to the left and to the right there was my bed, followed by a wall dresser and then the bathroom.

As far as work goes, I was responsible for providing financial management advice for US-funded projects with the Afghanistan Government. The Afghan war was still going on, so families were not allowed to come to the base due to the bombings and kidnappings. After being separated from my family for three and a half months, I was super excited to visit the family for Christmas after being gone oh so long.

A few days before Christmas, I was flying from Kabul, Afghanistan, to Dubai, UAE, onward to Dulles, VA, and then finally to good ole Nashville, TN. Since I had a nine-hour layover in Dubai, I decided to book a room at the Marriott so that I could buy my wife some 24K gold instead of the usual 14K gold jewelry that is sold at most jewelry stores, take a nice shower, eat a hot meal, and then relax a little bit before continuing the long journey back to Nashville.

The flight from Kabul to Dubai was smooth sailing. Feeling like a typical tourist, I picked up my suitcase and headed for the taxi stand outside. As I took two steps outside out of the Dubai Airport, the heat smacked me right in the face. It was H.O.T. Hot and dry! I quickly jumped into an air-conditioned taxi as fast as I could and was off to the Marriott hotel.

When I checked in, the receptionist upgraded me to a suite since I was a Marriott Gold member. Nice, Nice! Thank you, Marriot. As you can imagine, the suite was spectacular. It had a magnificent white garden tub, a full-size living room that was 300 $ft^2$, a spa style shower, and an extravagant bedroom. I dropped my suitcase off in the room, put my laptop and diplomatic passport in the hotel safe, and then went back downstairs to take a taxi to visit the Dubai GOLD Bazaar to buy a beautiful piece of jewelry for my love.

I jumped out of the taxi and was surrounded by store fronts full of gold, gold, gold, gold, and more gold along the street. When you Google Dubai Gold Bazaar you will see exactly why I was so blown away. I walked down a side street looking for a store that was willing to bargain because most of the stores on the main street don't like to bargain. These shop owners know that a lot of tourists feel extremely uncomfortable if they must negotiate a price after the owner tells them how much it costs. So they usually shout out a high price and then lean over to the tourist as they utter the golden phrase, "Just for you, sir or madam, I can sell it at X low price."

After going into a few of these stores and testing the lowest price that the stores were willing to sell their gold for, I strolled a few blocks behind the main road and into a store that had a nice hand-crafted bracelet that was unique and truly one of a kind. The shop owner pulled it out from underneath the glass and placed the bracelet into my hand. It was heavier than the traditional gold bracelets that you find in most malls. After feeling the weight of the necklace, I pulled it close to my eye to inspect the workmanship, which was stunning. I asked what the price was and the shop owner placed it on the scale to see how many grams it weighed and then multiplied that by the gold spot rate for the day, plus added the workmanship fee and then applied a small discount. I knew that in the United States it would have cost twice as much, but I could not act like a typical tourist and take the first discounted price offered.

While he was quoting the price, I started looking at other jewelry. I stated the price that I could pay for it and he started putting the bracelet into a beautiful jewelry box for me to impress my wife with. You get what you pay for. The price that you pay for quality things in your life will be forgotten throughout the passing of time, but the quality will last forever.

# How I Lost My Diplomatic Passport In Dubai

I really struggled to flag down a taxi from the main street. Despite it taking me ten minutes to finally get a taxi to stop, I was in a good mood because soon I would be back in my room enjoying that huge white garden bathtub. As soon as I entered the room, Rudoh was calling to check up on me.

After I soaked in the tub, I went to sleep for a few hours and awoke to a Beep, Beep, Beep sound coming from the alarm clock. I packed my bags, walked downstairs, and jumped into the taxicab for the Dubai Airport. Words could not express how excited I was to get back to the airport so that I could be home for Christmas to reunite with my wife and kids.

The taxicab driver pulled up to the Dubai International Terminal. I jumped out of the taxicab and headed straight towards the check-in counter. I walked up to the counter and reached into my backpack for my diplomatic passport, but

I could not find it. I searched and searched but it was nowhere to be found. By now you are probably thinking what I was thinking: I must have left my passport in the hotel safe!

I jumped back into a taxi to go back to the Marriott to check out the safe. I explained the situation to the hotel receptionist and when I checked the safe... the passport was Not There! I was shocked! I could not figure out where my passport could have disappeared to.

Although I had my regular tourist passport with me, it was no good because Dubai required a visa to enter and exit the country, along with an entry stamp. I pulled out my work phone and called the US Embassy to find out what I needed to do to fly out of Dubai since there was no way that immigration was going to let me out of the country without having a passport stamped with a visa. I was told that I would have to go around and collect nine different signatures from various ministries across all of Dubai.

Upon learning of my difficult circumstance, I phoned my wife and kids to tell them what happened. They could not believe it, but Rudoh was optimistic as usual that I would arrive just in time for Christmas. I was so disappointed in myself for losing my passport and, of all times, the day before Christmas.

The next morning, I woke up bright and early and headed straight to the Ministry of Foreign Affairs to collect the travel document that I needed to have approved. I had the document in hand and was told that I needed eight additional signatures, which were scattered across five different locations across the city. Deep down inside, I was thinking that this was going to be impossible, and to make matters worse, the offices would be closed the next day. You should have seen me; I was jumping in and out of taxi cabs to gather the necessary signatures as fast as possible.

By 12 p.m. I had gotten four signatures; I was really on a roll. The stars were lining up for me, I thought to myself. When I made it to the next station, there was a room full of eighty people waiting in line. Keep hope alive, I said to myself. I figured the line may be long, but it would move fast.

After an hour of waiting and the line barely moving, I began to become more and more pessimistic that things may not continue to play out like a scene in yet another movie where all ends well. After waiting for two and half hours, I finally got the 5th signature. It was now 2:30 p.m. and I needed three more signatures before all the offices closed at 4:30 p.m. I was starting to panic because even though I only needed three more, I was stuck in traffic.

As I was pulling up to the sixth location, I received a phone call from an unknown number. I hesitantly answered the phone, and it was the Marriott Hotel asking to speak to Michael Dillard. I said, "Speaking," and then the person on the line said that they had my diplomatic passport! I was like: What are they talking about, how can this be? I instantly redirected the taxi driver back to the Marriott.

When I entered the lobby, the receptionist walked up to me and handed me my diplomatic passport and told me to be careful with it. I asked her where she had found it, and she informed me that she called the taxicab company that had taken me to the Dubai airport to see if it had fallen in the car when I was getting out. Sure enough, that was exactly what happened! Could you believe it?

I was so relieved and ecstatic that I was going to get to spend Christmas with my wife and three little children. Deep down inside, I still think that I could have pulled off getting all eight signatures, I am just saying☺ FAVOR!

*You must keep your head up despite what is at stake. When you make a mistake, tell yourself that tomorrow it will all be better. In life you will make a mistake, but it is how you react to the mistake that will define who you will become.*

## My Bomb Scare in Afghanistan

Almost every week, when I turned the television to the news channel, it was showing images of a recent bombing or a story about a kidnapping in Afghanistan.

Fortunately for me, when I arrived in the country, these types of events were slowing down. I had been working in Afghanistan on large multimillion-dollar projects between the United States Government and the Government of Afghanistan for about six months when I learned how to make a handmade kite. A few colleagues and I went to the roof top of the U.S. Embassy to try them out. To our surprise the sky was filled with lots of colorful kites which were flown from the roof top of the local Afghans.

The next project that I was working on required that I review some of the Ministry of Finance's documents. For most documents, we could receive an electronic copy of them, but the documents that I needed to look at required that I speak with the Minister of Finance in person at his office. The thought of traveling from my heavily fortified building and riding down the streets of Kabul to meet someone was terrifying.

However, I chose this job assignment knowing what was expected of me and that one day I would have to travel outside of the USG compound. A security detail was put in place, and a time and date for the meeting were agreed upon for me to talk to the Afghan Minister in person.

The day had come, and I walked downstairs and met up with the security detail that would drive and escort me over to a Government of Afghanistan building. I fastened my bulletproof vest, tightened my helmet, and climbed into the vehicle. To my great surprise, all the pedestrian cars on the road were in good condition and the streets of Kabul were very well paved. The part of the city that I saw looked great, unlike what I had seen on the news, I must admit. For a minute, I forgot that I was in a country at war.

We pulled up to the building and hopped out of the vehicle. Someone escorted me into the building and into the room where I would be speaking with the Minister about a new USAID funded project. After waiting for a few minutes, I was informed that the Minister was running late due to a meeting that he was in. I sat and chatted with the local Afghan workers about how wonderful the city's infrastructure was before the meeting started. Deep down inside, my heart was beating fast. I wanted to get in and out ASAP before anyone knew that I was in the building. I did not want to sit around long enough for someone to realize that a living and breathing American was in the building.

The Minister came into the room about ten minutes later and as we were introducing ourselves, we heard a loud KABOOM! I was like: See, this is the exact reason why I did not want to leave that nicely fortified US Embassy compound surrounded by hundreds of soldiers and artillery. I immediately ducked down, not knowing if another bomb was going to go off. My security detail rushed in to get me and we exited the room. Since the KABOOM! noise sounded like it was about five miles away, we paused in the hallway to assess the situation.

Realizing that the explosion was way further out than we thought, it was determined that there was not an immediate threat at my location. We then moved into a safer room and continued with the meeting. Things were going well and then all of sudden, like in an action-packed movie scene, there were gunshots going off right outside the building and we could hear the Tat! Tat! Tat! Tat! Tat! Tat! Now at this point, the security team was like Weeee... GOT... to GO, and I was like YESSIR! Get me out of here ASAP before I pee on myself! Mr. Minister it was nice meeting you but I GOTs to GO!

Speeding up out of there and barely looking back, I was like: Get me home, Lord, please get me home! My office colleagues were tracking the situation and they were glad to see me back safe and sound.

It is okay to be fearful, but you cannot let FEAR control your life so much that you refuse to get out of your comfort shell. At times you will have to rely on your team to help you overcome certain obstacles at work or in your life. You must realize that you can do more as a team than as an individual.

# People Have Their Own Agenda

Have you ever wondered why someone would propose something that seemed to be so contradictory to what would be ideal? On several occasions, I found myself wondering why I must be the NO guy. Why can't people just choose to do the right thing that is needed for the situation at hand, instead of selling some story about why their plan needs to be approved—despite the fact that it will cause harm to others?

The more that I kept running into these types of situations, the more it became very clear to me. The reason people were making certain decisions that seemed off base and irrational, was because they had their own Agenda to satisfy, and you are literally a speed bump that is getting in their way. Thus, if you happen to find yourself in that position, remember that the person will do any and everything that they can to get you to conform to their decision.

I used to be so confused at times wondering why Larry was asking me to approve the document when all procedural requirements had not been completed. In that situation, Larry was intentionally giving me the document to approve with no intention of performing the prechecks. So, in essence, Larry put the burden on me to do the right thing, because if I cleared the document with my signature, he would implement his Agenda and blame me for it if something went wrong because I cleared the document. In these situations, when I asked about the prechecks, I usually got some story that basically says that the higher-ups want this done ASAP because it is Urgent. In these types of situations, I would then let Larry know that I would support this priority as soon as the prechecks were done so that I could clear it ASAP.

At other times people would create a story as to why their idea was so great and that I was the only person that prevented them from implementing it.

I did not let this disturb me.

Throughout my career, I have chosen to provide quality work as a mark of my professional brand that will follow me throughout the passing of time. Since I mark my work with excellence, people often say that if Michael signed off on it, then it is good to go. It has not always been easy choosing to do the right thing versus the convenient thing on behalf of others. But once I was able to identify and classify these types of actions, it kept me grounded knowing that they are trying to push their Agenda by any means necessary.

Remember that your name is your brand. When people mention your name in meetings, they are talking about your work, which is the brand that people associate your name with. You have a professional brand, so remember this when you are clearing the documents and signing the memos that require your personal branded signature.

# More Responsibility With Less Pay

It was time for me to apply for my next assignment. USAID categorized Afghanistan as a Critical Priority Country due to the dangerous working environment. As a benefit for working in Afghanistan, people received danger pay and the ability to apply for a preferred work assignment ahead of everyone else. Everyone saw this as the equivalent of having a golden ticket to work at some of the most sought-after Missions across the world. A lot of my colleagues were applying to work in Europe, Thailand, Peru, and the Philippines. I wanted to apply for an office director position, but my foreign service rank was three levels below that of a foreign service office director position of FS 1. By me doing a lot of great work over the years, I figured that I had a great chance of getting promoted from a foreign service rank of an FS 4 to an FS 3. The rule is that you can only apply for a position that is two grades above your rank without a waiver.

When I told people that I had applied to work in the Democratic Republic of Congo (D.R.C.) which was the 3rd poorest country in the world at that time, they looked at me like I was straight up CRAZY. However, in my Vision Plan I wrote down that I will apply to be an Office Director anywhere in the world so that I could get promoted faster. On top of this, I will have to endure twenty-four weeks of learning French from scratch at the torturous Foreign Service Institute that everyone dreaded.

A few weeks later, the promotion board promoted me to FS 3 and I was assigned to be the Office Director for the Financial Management Office in the Democratic Republic of Congo.

# If They Can Do It, You Can Do It!

Every time I received a promotion with a different title or more work responsibilities, I never doubted if I could do the job—and you should not either. I always told myself if s/he can do it, I can do it. Never let the fear of failure linger in your mind. My challenge to you is to believe in yourself and to push yourself to reach your fullest potential in your organization, life and/or marriage. If you look at people very closely, you will notice that the people that are in the positions one step higher than yours have made a few bad decisions, but overall, their work is stellar. The reason for a few bad decisions is that there are some things that they never got exposed to at their lower level. Higher-level positions require different skills and knowledge to resolve higher-level problems.

Think back to when you were a baby—the only issue for you at that time was that you needed and wanted something to eat. That was your one and only problem. You would not have the management and leadership skills to deal with a team of five people who have varying personalities if you had never managed a single person before.

However, the newly advertised team lead position requires that you lead a team of five people, but you have never supervised or managed a single person. Should you or should you not apply for the job? You should apply for the job but spend time reading books like Harvard Business Review on Leading People. Plus, you will need to understand what emotional intelligence really means for you and the impact on others.

As a new manager, you will do a lot of things very well but there will be a few employee-related issues that will be difficult for you to manage at first. Over time, you will gain the knowledge and experience of managing people as if you were a natural born supervisor. You should never limit what you can accomplish because of your current circumstance. Just like the weather, everything changes over time. If it can happen for them, it will happen for you.

*Well, one thing in life is that if it was that easy, everyone would be doing it. Your path to success will be and should be different from your neighbor's because we are not an exact clone of one another.*

## Time To Learn French

Twelve months in Afghanistan went by fast. I spent most of my time working out in the gym and Rudoh did the same. Upon the completion of my tour, I spent a few weeks with my family and friends, and then I was off to the infamous Foreign Service Institute to learn French. The FSI failure rate for people reaching a fluent conversational level of a 3/3 about any topic within six months was so high that they extended the training to seven months.

Since I only needed a very basic understanding level of 2/2, USAID signed me up for six months of language training. Having taken Spanish and being forced to obtain a 3/3 in thirty weeks, I knew that I was going to be in and out of FSI in about eighteen to twenty weeks. Rudoh and I did not want to uproot the children from school in Tennessee all the way to DC and then move to Kinshasa, D.R.C., weeks later, so they decided to remain in Tennessee. During this time, I would fly back and forth every other weekend.

Life is all about experiences. Some experiences or lessons are good, and other experiences are so bad that one would never want to repeat the experience again.

My first experience with learning Spanish was painfully bad because I did not know what I did not know. This time I was ready to tangle with French. I bought the 501 most used verbs book on Amazon and bought the audio version of the book 100 most used verbs by Sarah Retter on Audible. Finally, I Googled the 1,000 most used words in French and was ready to fail at saying the perfect sentence in French. Every time I was asked by the teacher to respond to his or her question in French, my goal was to fail forward as fast as possible until I made fewer and fewer mistakes day by day. I breathed, ate, and drank French. I was all in. Every day, I practiced conjugating the 100 most used verbs, read my list of 1,000 most used French words and listened to the 100 most French verbs audiobook seven days a week. By week six, I was able to understand most of what the teacher was saying to me in French. At week twelve, I could get my message across using very limited vocabulary words. At week sixteen, I was ready to test out because I knew that I was at the basic speaking and reading level of a 2.

Since it was the Christmas holiday, the school went on a break for a few weeks, which allowed me to fly back to Tennessee. I would wake up in the morning, drop our kindergartener and 3rd grader off at school and then practice, practice, practice French. When the school learned that I was an accountant who grew up within the area and now worked around the world, they asked me if I would be willing to talk to their students about their career prospects.

I remember the first day that I walked into the school, carrying thirteen flags that represented all the countries that I had personally visited. When I entered the classroom, the kids' faces would light up, especially if they recognized the flag of a country that they had visited or lived in before. Those were precious moments for me.

After the New Year holiday, the language school was back up and running. After twenty weeks of nonstop studying, I was allowed to take the French test. When I came out of the testing room, I knew that I had aced the reading and speaking tests. I happily waited the next day to receive my scores and was over the moon to receive a 2 in speaking and a 2+ in reading.

## On The Move Again

We decided to rent out our house in Antioch, TN, again instead of selling it so that we could continue to have someone pay our mortgage while the house increased in value year by year. Soon we were off to Kinshasa, the Democratic Republic of the Congo.

I was greeted by my wonderful sponsor as I exited baggage claims and then off to the parking lot and into the awaiting vehicle to take us to our new home. The ride from the airport to my house took two and a half hours. My sponsor explained that when it rained, the traffic backed up and no one abided by the traffic lights. It was literally every man and woman for themselves.

The next morning, I was picked up by a driver and taken to the office. I saw lots of street children sleeping on the side of the road, and people picking through the garbage and trash everywhere. I could not believe what I was seeing. I had never seen poverty like this before.

As the driver was turning into the USAID premise, she had to wait for the group of forty schoolchildren to move to the side. Along the street lay hundreds of small empty plastic bags that moments ago were filled with water.

Once inside the USAID premise, I got out of the vehicle, entered the building, and walked around until I found the section for the Office of Financial Management. I greeted everyone and then took my seat as a first-time Office Director. My sacrifice to leave Zambia two years early allowed me to become an office director sooner. The pay structure in the Foreign Service is different than in most organizations. Your pay is dependent on your rank. Thus, my rank at the time was two grades below the work that I was doing. As you know all so well by now, get the experience and the pay/promotion will follow. D'Largent, Mes Amis.

The 3,500 $ft^2$ house that we moved into had a private pool in the backyard. Since there was not much to do, we spent most of our time exercising. We took up jogging for twenty to forty minutes at a time outdoors for the first time after having children. Before moving to Kinshasa, we liked to do circuit training exercises instead of running on a treadmill or outside for many minutes at a time. We later took up boxing with a Congolese professional boxer. He was no joke; he whipped us into the best shape of our lives. In addition to the one-on-one boxing sessions, Rudoh and I would set up sixteen High Intensity Interval Training (HIIT) stations under the carport. During our workout sessions, we like to find our favorite 130 to 140 BPM songs and turn on the small but powerful Oontz Angle 3 Bluetooth speaker to get energized. We would warm up for five minutes and then the bell for the first forty-second exercise would go off. We would go all out for forty seconds at the first station, take a rest for twenty seconds, and then off to another station. On our rest day, we would go for a one-hour walk.

Soon the kids went from depending on me to use my FSI French to order food at the restaurant for them to the kids having full conversations with our housekeeper and placing their own food orders at the restaurants. Rudoh and I eventually learned that by walking or exercising together, it was the best way for us to spend time together and not forget Who We ARE as a couple.

*You must embrace failure as an opportunity to fail forward quickly in order to become the new version of yourself as fast as possible. Some people may choose to give up mid-journey.*

*By reading this far, YOU, however, are built like no other. You are the person that gets on the bike, falls off, and gets right back on the bike; riding onward to your destination while others fall down and stay there for the next twenty years, blaming others for their misfortune.*

# Terror Threat in Kinshasa, Democratic Republic Of Congo

Being a first-time Office Director comes with a lot of responsibility. As an Office Director you are not only responsible for your work, but the work of the twelve other people in your office, along with making sure that the US Government's $100 to $300 million programs to develop a country are being closely monitored. By having an if s/he can do it, I can do it attitude, I was not fearful of taking on more responsibility.

As part of my regional responsibilities, I had to make periodic visits to the Central African Republic just to check up on things there due to the fact that the Kinshasa Mission had financial management responsibility over it. Since I was more senior and held a prominent position in the Mission, I was often asked to serve as the Acting Deputy Mission Director (second person in charge of the Mission after the Mission Director). This was a very flattering experience because I had never envisioned myself being semi-responsible for the United States Government's development aid to the Democratic Republic of Congo.

President Kabila's term as president was overdue, but it kept being extended for one reason or another due to the Ebola pandemic, financial constraints, and security issues in the eastern part of the country. However, the international community was fed up and threatened sanctions if the elections did not go forward. As a result, the presidential election was finally given the green light by President Kabila to take place.

On one occasion, as the Acting Deputy Mission Director, I had to accompany the US Ambassador to his house for a meeting with two DRC Ministers in which USAID needed assistance resolving an outstanding dispute. When you are amid your Vision Plan, you will be elevated to levels and positions higher than what you could have dreamed up.

As we were going into the New Year, there was a lot of political tension, so we prepared our staff to call in every few hours over the weekend to report that all was well in their community. During this unstable political time, I was serving as the Acting Deputy Mission Director again when I received a few troubling calls one Sunday morning from several local employees who were trapped inside of a church after the local police had thrown tear gas into the church and blocked the doors to prevent anyone from being able to exit. This was one of the many scare tactics that was used to intimidate potential voters for the benefit of the other political party. Historically, in the weeks leading up to an election, police brutality is constantly used to stir the votes toward the preferred candidate. Those who openly protest are shot in plain sight or end up missing, never to be seen alive again.

One day we were told that we could not go into the office because there was a terror threat in Kinshasa. These were frightening times for everyone in the city because no one knew what was happening and whether the threat was real or just some story that had gotten out of hand. Meanwhile, the elections were scheduled to take place in a few months. Since the political climate was becoming very unpredictable, and with a history of violence in the past elections, the United States Government made a decision to evacuate all non-essential personnel out of the Democratic Republic of Congo and sent everyone back to Washington, DC.

After the elections were over and things quietened down, everyone returned to their posts. The promotion board recognized the great work that I had been doing and promoted me up an additional grade from FS 3 to FS 2. They could not promote me up to the grade of an Office Director because you had to work in your grade for at least two full years from the date of your last promotion before you were eligible for promotion again.

# Recognize Your All-Star Employees

I was watching TV at 10 p.m. when a call came in for an urgent action. I called a few people to gather the required documents to process the transaction after hours. I called person after person several times with no answer. Eventually, I reached someone that could help process the transaction at 11 p.m. It was not a coincidence that one of the highest performers was the person that answered the call.

I have seen this happen repeatedly. Those that perform at a high level will always perform at a high level. Those that perform well some days will disappoint on other days. You must always go out of your way to recognize high performers. If you don't recognize them, then you are telling everyone that if you do extra work, you will not be paid or recognized for it. People want to be thanked and recognized for performing at a high level—you should not take it for granted that that's just how the person is. If it was you who kept exceeding expectations, would you want to be recognized? If you never got recognized for performing at a high level, would you really keep doing more? People are your most important assets, so you must remember to appreciate and recognize them.

## You Do Not Have To Be Perfect

I have traveled the world and have been fortunate enough to work with a lot of people who hold very high positions in the United States Government (USG). When you are being introduced to these people, their official job titles (Ambassador, Mission Director, Chief of Mission, Chief of Party, Diplomat, Foreign Minister etc.) can be so intimidating at first. However, you must remember that these people are humans, just like us. There are things that you excel in and then there are things that you do not excel in, which is why they all have a staff of talented people who are paid to know what they do not know. You should not try to be perfect at everything that you do.

When you watch the news, some CEO or public official is being criticized for supporting some crazy project that failed. When these types of incidents are flaunted across the news, it is obvious that the person did not have enough information to know that it was a bad idea at the time when the decision was made. We can only know so much and understand the impact of our decisions at a later date, way into the future. Thus, everyone has their own personal limits about what they know. You should not be intimidated by people's titles. They make mistakes just like you and everyone else, because no one knows everything in life.

# South Africa—Year Five of the Vision Plan

It was time for me to bid again for my next onward diplomatic assignment. The Finance Office Director for Zambia was on the list, along with South Africa. The thought of going back to Zambia as an Office Director, and for four years this time, would be unheard of. South Africa, however, was one of the largest Regional Missions in the world with financial management responsibility for Angola, Botswana, Eswatini, Lesotho, Namibia, South Africa, and Prosper Africa. We figured that someone coming from a Critical Priority Country would choose South Africa over Zambia since it was one of the very few Senior Foreign Service/Highest financial management positions in the world, managing a staff of forty people and overseeing a yearly development budget of $800 million.

To my surprise, someone chose Zambia over the South Africa Office Director position. I was not expecting this, but I did put that I wanted to work as a Regional Controller after my first Office Director assignment in my Vision Plan. Rudoh and I knew that the competition was going to be high for the South Africa position since the International Schools were some of the best in the world and the infrastructure in Johannesburg and Pretoria were as developed as in the United States. I put South Africa as number one on my list, despite being told that they already had someone as their number one choice. At one point, someone even told us that we had just wasted our number one choice by ranking South Africa first because someone they knew already had a handshake for the position.

But you know by now that Rudoh and I always follow our hearts. Being told that I was not the Mission's number one choice didn't bother us, because we have always believed that we would end up where God wants us to be, no matter what.

Like clockwork, Rudoh started telling people that we were going to be assigned to South Africa, even though the assignment board was not going to meet for at least another two months.

Three days before the assignment list was out, Rudoh told me that she saw the list in her dream and that it had my name next to South Africa. Once the deadline for assignments was supposed to be released, I stayed up every night waiting to see where we would go to next. For some unknown reason, the assignment list was late and did not come out as scheduled in mid-December. I kept staying up late, checking my phone for updates on my assignment. Rudoh told me to stop stressing and staying up late for no reason. The joke among friends of ours was that Rudoh was showing up in South Africa with bags in hand, regardless of what the assignment list showed.

It was time for us to fly to the United States for the Christmas holidays, and I realized that the assignment list was only going to come out after the holidays were over. It felt great to be back to see all of the holiday decorations. We decided to drive up to Murfreesboro, to visit a wonderful church couple that had touched our marriage so much. They were always sharing some very precious marriage counseling lessons during the Sunday married couple's lessons at Mt. Zion Baptist Church in Antioch, TN.

Since the Walmart in Murfreesboro sold a lot of MTSU college apparel, I decided to drive up to Murfreesboro an hour early to buy an MTSU hat before visiting our friends. I was in the toy aisle, looking at the newly released games, when I received a phone call from a colleague who told me congratulations. Congratulations! On What? You got South Africa. God's FAVOR! Of all times, Walmart did not have any MTSU hats for sale. To celebrate the great news, I bought myself a caramel Twix. It really is the best candy bar in the world.

Right before we reached our friends' house in Murfreesboro, Rudoh told me to stop the car. As soon as the car came to a stop, she jumped out and started running in the middle of the street. It was twenty degrees Fahrenheit at the time, and it was raining. The kids and I were confused. We did not know what to do. We eventually caught up with her and I asked what had happened. She said that she was so full of joy and excitement that she had to run it out to praise God for being so faithful to us. We had a great fellowship at our friends' house to cap the day off.

After spending time with more of our friends and family, our holiday vacation was over. We were back in the D.R.C., taking time to enjoy the tasty grilled goat meat and prawns before it was time to pack up and move to South Africa.

# On The Road Again

We arrived in South Africa and moved straight into a beautiful two-story house with a pool.

The next day, Rudoh and the girls were picked up by a friend that we had served with at our first post in the Dominican Republic. While they were out doing their thing, M.J. and I decided to walk the neighborhood to get to know our surroundings. We stopped at a nice local restaurant a few blocks from our house named Three Ducks/Les Trois Connards to see what we could find to eat. They were so happy to meet me and M.J. that they decided to take a picture of us and post the photo on their Facebook page here.

Living in South Africa was truly a dream come true. South Africa is a very developed country and has some of the best local restaurants that I have ever enjoyed throughout my travels. Whenever there was a long three-day weekend, my family and I would fly to Port Elizabeth and rent an Airbnb house that's twenty steps from the beach.

One Thanksgiving, Rudoh fried a turkey the Wednesday before Thanksgiving and wrapped it up in aluminum foil and packed it in our carry-on bag to protect it throughout our flight from Johannesburg, South Africa, to Port Elizabeth, South Africa. I am happy to report to you that the turkey arrived safe and sound. We made macaroni and cheese, cooked some vegetables, and then had one of the best Thanksgiving dinners of all times, listening to the ocean waves crash against the beach. It was such a peaceful and relaxing moment. You should try it one day.

From a work perspective, I was in one of the top overseas financial management positions at USAID. I was the Director for the Regional Office of Financial Management with the responsibility of providing financial management oversight for USAID's development projects in Angola, Botswana, Eswatini, Lesotho, Namibia, and South Africa.

With the help of the forty people that I managed; we were able to accomplish a lot. They really made my job memorable. There was not a day that passed that I did not look forward to going into the office to speak with my team. When you work with great people, the work is easy.

When I sat down in my office, I would often look out onto the office floor and reflect on my life. Wow, I started from the bottom and now I am here! I kept thinking about how much of an impact Upward Bound had on me. I told myself that whenever I was in the United States, I would deliver motivational speeches at some of the Upward Bound programs in order to inspire the next version of me to never give up, because success is just around the corner.

I officially joined the South Africa Toitus Toastmasters Club so that I could learn how to become a better public speaker. I could already see the difference from when I gave my first speech to when I gave my third speech, which was a powerful one. I titled the speech, 3, 2, 1, Action! Since its presentation, people keep telling me how inspired they were from that one speech and how it influenced them to make vital changes in their life, which allowed them to meet prior goals that they had set for themselves.

When COVID-19 became a worldwide pandemic, it forever changed everyone's lives. The world went from putting on a suit and dress in the morning and then driving to the office for work, to getting up out of bed and putting on a blouse or dress shirt on top, while wearing pajamas or shorts below and then logging into a Zoom meeting for work from the kitchen or the living room. In addition, parents became overnight schoolteachers who were responsible for helping their children with the lesson for the day since schools had to close abruptly.

Since South Africa has been one of the most severely COVID impacted countries in the world, I was seeing first-hand how COVID was affecting the lives of my staff and their family. I constantly called each one of them to check up on them because I knew that the work would always be there, but that people are irreplaceable. I encouraged each of my employees to take short rests throughout the day for a mental break or take a short walk every few hours in order to lower the stress that they were experiencing due to the increased workload or the loss of someone close to them.

After work, Rudoh and I would take thirty- to forty-five-minute walks and discuss our life and our Vision Plan. One topic that kept coming up was if our oldest child should go to High School overseas or go to High School in the United States. We eventually decided that it would be best for us to move to the United States so that she could have an American High School experience and get to know all aspects of living in America. In addition, she would be able to participate in all the extracurricular activities that she desired, go to basketball and football games, and most importantly, develop long-lasting friendships.

The decision to move back to the United States despite me being in such a high-profile position was an easy one to make. In life, everyone in the family makes sacrifices in order to allow others to succeed. Throughout my professional career, my family happily moved from Tennessee to Washington, DC, to the Dominican Republic, to

Zambia, back to Tennessee, to the Democratic Republic of Congo, and then to South Africa. At this moment in my life, it was time for me to make a sacrifice so that my daughter could enjoy life in the country that she was born in but barely lived in. I am forever appreciative to have worked with such a wonderful group of people throughout all of my overseas USAID assignments.

As soon as we touched down in the United States, we had a long list of things that we had to take care of ASAP.

Day one to day three were spent looking for a car that we really liked and could afford to pay cash for. Days four to nine were spent looking for a house to buy and make doctors' appointments. On days eleven to thirteen we were off to Knoxville, TN, to meet up with family. Days fourteen to seventeen had us off to Virginia Beach to visit more family. Between days eighteen and twenty we rested. Days twenty-one to day twenty-four, we finalized getting the children registered for school. And on days twenty-five to thirty, Rudoh and I completed the last few edits to the book.

Since being back in the United States, we have had numerous people come up to us in a hotel lobby or on an airplane to compliment Rudoh and me on how well behaved our children act. It is always an honor to get such wonderful feedback about our children. Early in our marriage, Rudoh and I decided to practice positive micro reinforcement parenting. We would only buy our children extravagant toys and clothes after they finished doing five hours of educational learning on www.ixl.com for the week and completed their chores. Any time they misbehaved we would explain to them why the behavior was not appropriate, and that people were always watching what they do.

Eventually, if a flight attendant complimented us on how quiet they were or how they did not make a big mess on the plane, our children would pretend not to hear what they said. However, as soon as we got off the plane, they would remind us how great the flight attendant said they were and hint at us buying them a toy they wanted. ☺

*No matter where you are in life, career, or marriage, you can always achieve more with positive thoughts and actions. Anything is possible, trust me, I know ☺.*

# PART TWO

## MY FAVORITE MOTIVATIONAL PHRASES

# Build Your Vision Plan Today!

Every year, Rudoh and I set a one-year, three-year, and five-year Vision Plan. If we never took the time out of our busy lives to say, Hey, where do we want to be in one year, we would not have achieved what we have thus far. Wandering around the forest without a map is not a pleasant experience. This is true in life. You must have a map or a Vision Plan to guide your steps.

As an example, our Vision Plan would typically go like this: Michael will focus on writing a book in year one, Rudoh will release her book in year three, and we will speak at various conferences together during the summer. In year five we will buy a new house in South Africa on the beach—cash. Because of this, I am working where I want to work, doing what I want to do, contributing to my TSP 401k account, and maxing out our IRA accounts. This was not an accident. Without a Vision Plan, we would have gotten lost several times in the forest of life.

Our actual Vision Plan was as follows: In 2014 we planned for me to go work in Afghanistan in August of 2015 and then the following year seek an Office Director position at one of the least sought-after locations. We made this decision so that I would have a better chance of getting promoted since I would be one of the very few people in a lower grade managing and leading an office in a "hardship" country. For the next assignment, we agreed that we would go to the country that had the best school system since our kids were getting older. I also wanted to serve in another Office Director position but this time at a Regional Mission, which covered several of the smaller countries around it.

In 2017, I was assigned as Office Director in the Democratic Republic of Congo, one of the poorest countries in the entire world. In 2018, I was promoted just as we had planned, and in 2019, I was assigned to a Regional Mission as an Office Director—just like we planned it.

Your Vision Plan will allow you to achieve things that you would never have thought possible. If you do not have a Vision Plan, then you are walking in the middle of a dark forest with no hope of ever getting out. You cannot follow the path that others take in the forest of life because their destination and path are not the same as yours.

I have been able to accomplish a lot of things in my life by having a Vision Plan that covers where I will be in one year, three years, and five years out. I did not try to build a plan that is further than five years out because life changes every five years. I stumbled upon having a Vision Plan when I lost my job but had just completed my MS in Accounting because I wanted to change my career. I applied for overseas government jobs because I wanted to work close to Zambia. My one-year Vision Plan allowed me to become a US Diplomat. So, I thought to myself, what would happen if I planned my life in one- , three- and five-year phases? What other great things could happen?

Since I joined USAID in 2010, I have gotten every single assignment that I bid on, such as getting Zambia, which was the reason I became an Accidental Diplomat. Then I wanted a promotion, so I went to Afghanistan, then I wanted to be an

Office Director and I also wanted to learn French so I went to the Democratic Republic of Congo, and then next I wanted to be an Office Director at one of the largest Missions and be at a place with great schools for my children.

At the time of writing of this book, I am an Office Director in South Africa, in one of the largest Missions covering six countries, and my children are going to one of the best International Schools in all of Africa. I only share my Vision Plan with my wife because what God has in store for me will be different from what God has in store for others. People will criticize your Vision Plan because they think that you are supposed to take the same path as they take in this journey that we call life. However, there is more than one way to get to Washington, DC, from Antioch, TN. As long as you reach your destination, that is what matters in life, no matter how slow or fast it takes for you to reach your destination.

## You Are The Chosen One

Always remember that the company chose YOU out of all people, because they believe in YOU, so you need to start believing in YOU if you ever have a doubt of belonging.

On one occasion, I was sitting across from the Minister of Finance, when a burst of energy and joy hit my forehead. I was so astonished to be sitting in front of a Minister whose colleagues saw me as the sole representative of the United States Government. It was at that moment that I reflected on my path up until this point; my words were going to represent a whole country because I was the only American Diplomat in the room. These Foreign Ministers had no idea about my past or how long I had been a US Diplomat. Thus, you don't have to fake it until you make it. You are who you say you are.

When your VISION Plan puts you in higher and higher positions, that means that You are the chosen One for that job at that time. No one else can take your spot. Thus, take pride in your accomplishments. Do not let negative comments distract you from your moment. There have been countless times when others have taken my advice in a technical area where they know better than me. This is because I was the chosen one at that very moment, who was destined to add value to that particular development project.

I have learned to believe in the moment. If you believe it, you achieve it. If I can do it, you can do it. Take the time to write down on a piece of paper what your one-year, three-year, and five-year career goals are. Also, work out what your one-year, three-year, and five-year financial plans are. This powerful tool is what has allowed my family and me to achieve dreams unimaginable to most people.

I have also learned that you should not take for granted what you have accomplished in your life. I know that there were many more people who applied for the position that I have, but the company selected me. Thus, I am the chosen one. I truly believe that it was my preparation, knowledge, and experience that allowed me to have the job. I am the chosen one and I do not think twice when I must make an unpopular decision. I make decisions based on what I know is the correct solution at that moment. It is true that the former boss may have done it a different way, but I am the person who is responsible for providing a solution that will resolve the current problem.

I remember working at a post and people kept telling me that they never had to do things according to the policy. A few colleagues made the comment that I should lower my standards because the staff are not capable of performing at the Agency standard. I was shocked by this. I had two choices. I could lie to the staff and tell them that they were performing at a B and accept their poor work, or I could reject the work and let them know that it was below standard and thus a D. I chose the latter because I was the person chosen to be the Financial Management Office Director for that country. Thus, I brought in experienced staff from other Missions to work side by side with them. Eventually, the staff understood that it was possible to follow the Agency policies and complete the work in a timely manner.

Later on, the Mission received a letter of gratitude for correcting years of unreconciled transactions with the US Treasury. I would rather have someone complain about me for doing my work the correct way versus doing it the wrong way. I know that I am the person at the moment that was chosen and thus I trust in my abilities to get the job done. You need to be confident that your way will work and is the best for them at that moment, otherwise you would not be there. You must also remember that people won't recognize the value that you bring until you are gone, so don't expect any praise from them while you are there. The price paid for quality is long forgotten ten years later.

# When It Smells Like A Fish It Is Probably A Fish

Have you ever had someone tell you that you should be careful of a particular person because they lie, talk down on others, or mistreat people? They are telling you this because someone learned this the hard way. Well, this is true of some people. I remember seeing a colleague complain about a person in the office. They said that the person disrespected them. As a neutral observer, you may give the person that was disrespectful the benefit of the doubt that they were having a bad day. That is, until you and the person are working together on a project and all is well—until it isn't.

You want to make a change to the report, but the other person insists that there is no need to update the report. So, you decide to compromise and not make a big fuss over the update. During the presentation of the project, people are in love and making wonderful comments about the great work. At the end of the presentation, everyone claps, and you open the floor up for questions. A colleague asks you to go back to slide ten and makes a comment about the data being inaccurate. Your colleague then turns to you and says that you made the mistake and insisted on not working with them to vet the numbers and says that you are always doing things at the last minute, which causes inaccurate reporting. Just like your other colleague, you too have been bitten by the dog. People are indeed who they say they are. If they disrespect other people, it is only a matter of time before they will disrespect you too.

# Coach To Lead

You cannot do it all yourself. As I moved into higher and higher diplomatic positions, I realized that my job was no longer to do the job, but to motivate and teach others to do the job. As a diplomat, you move every two to four years to a new country, where you are working with a new staff of ten to twenty employees on average. It typically takes about one year for you to understand your portfolio and grasp the do's and don'ts within the local culture and the business norms of the Mission.

The number of issues that I experienced early on as a supervisor became daunting. Every email or phone call that I received from members of my staff was about a problem that they wanted me to fix. I would wake up early in the morning and respond to a few emails before I arrived at work. I would work through lunch, arrive home, eat dinner, and then dive into work again after dinner. I would go to bed thinking about all of the many problems that I had to solve the next morning.

After taking a course in leadership training, I received four one-on-one coaching sessions. It was right then that I had my ah ha moment. What if I could become a coach for each of the forty employees in my office—what would happen? Well, the results were startling. I started to receive fewer and fewer emails about a problem that my staff needed me to resolve. This observation led me to focus on coaching employees, instead of directing them on how to do or resolve the issue at hand. In addition, I am taking the accredited International Coach Federation (ICF) training to become an executive leadership coach. The personal benefit of this strategic change in leadership was that ten to twenty fewer issues were coming to me each day.

For example, when I get a call about a problem that an employee is facing, I help them to identify the issue and the impact that the issue has on the Mission or the person. Then I ask them what solutions are appropriate for the situation. I help the employee to think through a few ideas until they settle on the solution that works best. A huge benefit of this coaching style is that the employee feels empowered knowing that You as a supervisor support THEIR ideas. When you are managing a large office, there is no way that you will have 100% of the details available to you. The people that are closest to the problem are in the best position to provide a solution to the problem with a little assistance now and then from their supervisor. Once you implement a coaching style instead of a "do this" leadership style, all of your employees will be able to take on higher levels of responsibility as they gain more experience resolving issues on their own. The direct benefit for you is that you will have more time to focus on the big picture, which is to implement the company's strategic vision.

## Learn To Fly

Every problem is an opportunity for you to rise higher.

Suppose that you have a big problem, and you are so stressed because you don't know how to resolve it and it is making you look bad. You start to get all fussy with your colleagues because of your big problem. You can keep fussing about it until you run away from the big problem or you can choose to take on the new challenge. Once you decide to sit up straight and make a determination to take on the challenge, you will be very nervous. However, eventually you will conquer the big test that is in front of you. The next time that you encounter that very same problem, you will simply handle it with ease. I am confident of this because you have wings that were made to work at a higher level than others. Thus, you are flying at a higher altitude than you were before. Those old problems that used to get you all frustrated and upset look like tiny ants from the altitude that you are currently flying at. Fly high, my friend, fly high.

## Everything Will Not Be Easy

If you failed at something twice, would you give up or keep trying? Well, this was my predicament. I had applied for a higher-level position because my sales were in the top tier. I had consistently hit my sales number and had routinely shared my best practices with my colleagues.

So, when a position opened up looking for someone to work on the one-time large orders that a business needed, I figured that I was the man for the job. I prepped for the interview by having my wife ask me all types of interview questions. Here is a very important tip, so take note: you cannot expect to pass a job interview if you have not practiced answering their questions while also including your great accolades and skills that they did not directly ask you about. The person that just interviewed in front of you is a veteran and thus has been practicing nonstop, so don't leave it to chance to get that raise. I thought that the interview went well, so I was excited about the thought that in a week I would be in a higher position.

The following week, I was informed that I did well in the interview, but I had not made the rounds to get to know the group that I would be working for. Lesson learned the hard way; you must do the job to get the job. I immediately went around introducing myself to the group of managers and made it my priority to sit down with the new sales reps to help them increase their IT sales by upselling software and warranty services.

A few months later, another position was available, so I applied and interviewed again. This time, I had done the courtesy round of getting to know people and letting them know who Michael is. I was more than ready for the interview questions that they were going to throw at me. The next week, I got a message to come to the post-interview room and walked into the room full of pride and joy because I knew that I was the best person at that time for the job. Well, I did not get the job, folks, because someone else had been in line trying to get the job before me. I was devastated. I could not believe my ears. I told myself to keep my head up because that job would be mine one day. I applied a third time and got the job. You must tell yourself that if it was that easy, everyone would be doing it.

## Head Start

Have you ever watched a four-person relay race and started cheering as the baton was being handed over to the next teammate to continue the race? If the team that you are cheering for is in second or third place at the midway point, you are very optimistic that your team will catch up and overtake everyone to be declared the winner, right?

In life, there are people who have a head start. They come from a rich family, went to the best schools growing up, had nice paying internships, and were offered a prominent job before graduating from college. However, this will not always be the case for most people. If you do not have a head start, you just need to focus on the finish line and look past the fact that others are ahead of you. When you start from the bottom, you build courage and stamina along the way that will become your head start later in life.

*In the race of life, when someone has a head start but they are still in eyesight, lace up your running shoes and get into the race. You are a winner! The victory is yours to grab.*

# Why The Grass Is Greener On the Other Side

Remember that time when you were driving down the road and you passed by one of your neighbor's houses and noticed how green their yard was? The grass was magnificently cut and pristine. You thought: If I had that grass in my yard, my house would look amazing.

What would you do to have that same grass in your yard? What sacrifices would you make? Would you be willing to wake up at 5:30 a.m. to water the grass, sprinkle fertilizer on the yard every month to give it that nice rich color, and cut the grass exactly one inch every five days? Plus, once a year you have to penetrate the surface by poking holes into the depths of your yard so that it can breathe properly. A lot of the change that is happening is occurring under the surface where no one can see, but the benefits are outstanding.

Is this something that you are willing to do to have the same results as your neighbor or coworker? It is not a coincidence that the results show up years after the first part of the work was completed. It takes a few years before the soil is at the right PH level for your grass to grow everywhere in your yard without a single open patch. Yes, the grass is greener on the other side, but you must be willing to put in the work no matter the day or time. The great thing about life is that today is the best day to fertilize yourself from within so that you too can become greener and more vibrant in the future. At first, people will not notice all of your internal changes, but the following season they will notice that something about you just looks different.

# Catching Fish

I was walking along the beach in Port Elizabeth, South Africa, with my wife one early morning on vacation. We were so close to the surf that our feet could gently touch the water. The water was nice and cool. We kept walking beachside and noticed a fisherman with his long fishing pole peering off into the water. We wondered if they were really able to catch fish being so far away from the water. Onwards we went and saw a few more people putting bait on their lines and tossing the line out into the sea to try to catch a fish.

Not long after, we came across a group of people from the Middle East or Northern Africa. Inside their bucket lay a few small fish. They noticed the joy and excitement on our faces and asked me if I wanted to give it a try.

"Of course, I would," I said excitedly.

The fisherman took his knife out and cut a piece of bait and put it on the hook. I took the fishing rod and walked out into the surf until the water was knee deep and I flung the line back behind me and then forward into the water. The line was left to run so that it would carry the bait out to sea among the waves. I slowly walked back to the beach shore and then started chatting with the fisherman about the area and how often he comes out to fish. As he was telling me about the dolphins that normally pass by in the evening, I felt a tug on the line. I looked at the fisherman for guidance and he told me to close the line. So, I pushed the side button and the line stopped making noise. We were all quiet for a few seconds wondering if there was a fish nibbling on the bait. We were very still. Then I felt a big tug and stumbled forward a few steps. I pulled the rod up quickly at a 90-degree angle so that I could hook the fish. Bingo, it worked!

I started to slowly pull the line in so that I could see what I caught. After about forty-five seconds, I started to get tired from pulling the fish in, but I did not want to stop and risk the fish coming off the hook. I kept reeling in the fishing line until the fish was eventually on the shore. You must be willing to try new things in life when the opportunity presents itself because you never know what you will catch until you try.

## Tomorrow Is A Liar

No one is promised tomorrow. I know you will lose weight tomorrow; you will exercise tomorrow; you will save money tomorrow. Why tomorrow and not today? Stop making tomorrow a liar out of you. Do it today or don't do it. You are what you do today.

If you exercise today, then tomorrow you will exercise. If you save money today, then tomorrow you will save money. If you don't do it, then you will never do it. In order to finish something, you have to start it. It is not the other way around where you are finished before you have started. Make action your new friend. Say that you are going to do something and then immediately name the verb that will make the action happen. I want to lose weight, I will ACTION/walk for thirty minutes five days in a row. I want to save money, I will ACTION/transfer $100 into a Vanguard S&P 500 fund. Don't make yourself a liar tomorrow.

Life is full of so many distractions and things that are out of our control. If you plan to walk tomorrow and it rains, will you walk in the rain for thirty minutes or say, I will walk tomorrow? Will you really do it tomorrow if you did not do what you said you would do yesterday? Will the excuse of the day continue to determine your tomorrow? Choose the verb and make the verb past tense. I walked for thirty minutes today.

I opened an IRA account today. I cooked a healthy meal today. I completed the ACTION TODAY ☺.

## Squeeze The Lemon

Your life may be bad now. You may not have gotten that promotion that you thought that you were going to get, but don't let it ruin who you are on the inside and the outside. Take the lemon that you received today, squeeze it out, add hot water and sugar, and make it into something tasty, like lemonade.

When you show up at work excited and full of hope, people around you take notice of your presence. They will see that you did not let the misfortune define who you are. An event does not make you; you make the event. Learn from your experiences and use them to make you a better person today. Take a bad situation and turn it into a positive one. You can always learn something from a mistake or a temporary setback.

No one in baseball bats 1000 out of 1000. However, you cannot hit what you don't swing at. Did you know that in the game of baseball, that if you can hit the ball four out of every ten times at bat, you are deemed an all-star player? In baseball, you can literally fail 60% of the time and succeed 40% of the time. You would be considered a walk into the hall of fame.

You will fail at some point in time if you are growing your talent and skills—everyone fails, thus you are not alone. However, it is those that choose to go back up to the plate and swing at another chance who will reap the benefits. In due time, you too will hit your goals out of the park as long as you are willing to turn your lemon into lemonade.

# Enjoy The Ride

Sometimes in life, we are too worried about getting to our next promotion or buying the latest gadget that has just come out. We must remember to pause for a moment and enjoy the scenery. There are no guarantees that you will return to where you came from. The joy of reaching your destination is all about what you saw, learned, and experienced getting there.

I know that throughout the many vacations to numerous countries and work promotions that I have obtained that there were several moments that really counted.

I remember driving down the road until I came across a long winding road where several cows were grazing along the road. It was such a wonderful sight to see because it was unexpected. It was nature at its best. The cows were moving at their own pace, while we humans were hurrying along the highway to get to our next vacation spot. The fact that I am writing about the cows shows you how vivid the scene was. I also enjoy watching windmills spin along the highway as I drive through the countryside because it shows the power of energy in motion. As you progress in life, don't forget to enjoy the little things that made the journey special.

## You Cannot Eat Everything That You See

I have enjoyed so many things in life that most people can only afford to dream of. I have experienced so many one-of-a-kind vacations because I learned very early in life to save my money and to only buy what I really want and not listen to false promises made by ads in the media.

However, I will buy a $100 pair of dress shoes, fly business class, or spend extra money to buy organic food. I, like many others, want to enjoy the best that life has to offer, but only within reason. I have learned through experience that buying a cheap pair of shoes will be okay at first, but twelve months later, those cheap shoes will be in the back of my closet, hoping to see the light of day one more time. When you invest in quality shoes, you will not need to have three pairs of black shoes in the back of the closet that are faded or ripped. If you want to smell good all day, then buy the cologne/perfume from the store and stop buying that imitation stuff because it will not last as long.

You will smell good for ten minutes and then it will turn into something else.

I have learned to take things nice and slow in life. I have flown business class and yes, it is enjoyable. However, if I am on a two-hour flight, that extra room would be nice, but it is not going to drastically change my flying experience. I can save the $300 upgrade fee and invest in the stock market for my early retirement, which will be way more satisfying. Do you really need the newest phone, car, or newly released shoes? Learn to love what you love, do what you love and let the others enjoy what they love. You cannot eat everything that your eyes see because your stomach will burst, and you will go bankrupt.

# Do Not Let Jonah In Your Boat

In life, you will be called upon for help. A friend may call you and ask you for a favor, a neighbor may need to borrow something, or the store clerk may tell you about a recent setback. Who will you choose to help and at what cost?

If you are sailing along in your boat and you come across a person that needs you to tug their boat up to the riverbank where the current is calm, you can let them paddle at their own speed or you can tie their boat to your boat. You choose the latter. Along the way, you see a person waving their arms from the deck of their boat. Do you stop to see what they want, or do you keep going? You decide to stop to find out what the person wants. They ask for some fuel because they ran out. So, you take your spare gas container and empty it into their fuel tank. You then ask the person how they ran out of fuel. They tell you that they left the dock on fumes but hoped that a generous person such as yourself would come along and help them.

The person thanks you and tells you how grateful they are and that you will be well rewarded for having such a great big heart.

You begin your journey back towards the riverbank with the other boat still in tow and you come across three people floating in the water with life vests on. The person in the boat that you are tugging tells you to keep going; there is no time to stop because he will be late if you do. You pass up one person, but the second person tells you that you are her only hope. The third person tells you to keep going and that they will swim ashore. You let passengers two and one in your boat. The person in the boat that is being tugged along is mad and giving you the eye. You ask the other two people what happened and why the third person didn't want to get into the boat. They tell you that they were in the third person's boat and that it capsized because it was too small to hold their weight and that the boat sank.

Be careful of how much you are willing to take on because of other people's poor planning, mistakes, and neglect, because soon it will be you in the water looking for help along with the others.

On the plane, they tell you to put on your oxygen mask before you put on your child's oxygen mask. They tell you this because you are in the best position to save your child instead of the reverse scenario of having your child put their mask on and then having to reach up to help you with yours.

# Level Up

In life, we enjoy things differently as we age. The person at age twenty is very different from the thirty-year-old version of ourselves. As we go up another level, every ten years we take on a new identity based on our lived experiences. Who will you be at level three, four, or five? We must be the person that we strive to be today. As we go up a level, we have less time to achieve our dream.

I once wanted to run a 21K marathon. I knew that running for more than thirty minutes was tough for me because I get bored, and I start thinking to myself that thirty minutes is better than nothing. However, on the other hand, I say to myself: if I don't do it this week, then when will I do it? I eventually signed up to run the Johnson Crane 21K marathon in Johannesburg, South Africa. As soon as I crossed the finished line, I realized that I had reached another level in life.

Sometimes, on seeing so many obituaries on the news and on social media, I wonder what else the person planned to accomplish in life before they ran out of time. What more did they have to share? Before I reach my final level, I want to have completed everything in life that I dreamed of accomplishing and achieving.

# PART THREE

# Generational Wealth

Like most people working hard each and every day to earn a living, I only focused on how much money I would make this year so that I could buy all the wants that my eyes desired.

After returning from a wonderful rest and recuperation break in Zambia, I started to get curious about how much money I needed to save up so that I could stop working and retire. I knew that I could expect to receive Social Security, money from my US Government Pension, money from my TSP/401K account, and money from my individual retirement account. So, I spent hours upon hours reading up and learning about the newest retirement and investing options.

Once I developed my personal finance foundation, I started doing the retirement calculations of how much a pension is worth; how much my TSP/401K account will be worth after years of investing in my employer-sponsored retirement account; how much I will receive from Social Security and its worth and finally; how much my IRA account will be worth and how much can I safely withdraw over a thirty-year timeframe.

When I finally finished doing all of these calculations, I was Oh, So Happy! After working twenty years as a US Diplomat, I will have the equivalent of $1.5 million dollars for my retirement, which does not include the value of my TSP/401K account and my Individual Retirement Account (IRA). Say What! Not only did I become a US Diplomat by accident, but I also have an Accidental Millionaire retirement payout for my willingness to travel the world in order to represent the United States of America.

Over the past few years, I have been asked by several people to provide financial planning or retirement planning advice. I will share a few of my personal financial secrets that have worked for me, my family, and some of my friends. Please consult with a professional financial advisor because I am not a financial advisor. I am only sharing what has worked for me and my family. Everyone's financial situation is different and thus I am not liable for any loss.

# What Is Income Insurance?

What type of insurance do you buy in the event that you are in a car accident? Car insurance. What type of insurance do you buy if you need to have medical treatment? Medical insurance. What type of insurance do you buy if you are married and your spouse's yearly income of $40,000 or lifetime earnings of $1,200,000 ($40,000 x 30 years) is suddenly gone due to an unexpected death? Income Insurance or Term Life Insurance.

Immediately after my wife and I got married and had our first child, we knew that we needed to buy Term Life Insurance to protect our income in the event that something happened to one of us. Even when I was unemployed, we kept paying our term insurance so that our children would not suffer financially in the event that one of us passed away. If you are living in a three-bedroom house with two children who enjoy playing sports, what will happen to them if one of their parents suddenly dies? How will you keep paying the mortgage for the next twenty or so years? How will you pay for childcare and continue to take your children to practice for the next ten years or so? This will be a big lifestyle change if you do not have term life insurance. So, I tell people to buy about twenty-five times their yearly salary so that you and your children do not have to suffer in the event a spouse dies.

If you look at the back of your Church magazine, you will find someone selling insurance most of the time. We looked at the back of Mt. Zion's Trumpet magazine and contacted Bobby Thomas Jr. when we bought our term life insurance. I know you have an extra $50 a month to secure the financial legacy of your family. Don't put off till tomorrow what will secure your family's financial future today.

## Don't Be Car Rich

I made the mistake of walking into a car dealership and buying a nice, sparkling new car that was worth way more money than I had in the bank.

Like a lot of men and women, I was the main attraction riding around in my modern four-door, mid-size car. Then, after a few years, the new car smell went away, and the car turned into a heavy anchor that I had to carry around everywhere that I went. The debt was weighing me down. I had signed my name to not five years of debt, but for six years of paying for something that loses value every year. I swore never to make that mistake again.

How can you spend more on your car today than you plan to save in your retirement account when you can no longer work? You cannot work forever.

My wife and I came up with a rule. Yes, we wanted to drive a nice car without mechanical problems, but not at the expense of going into tons of debt just to show off to friends and neighbors.

Here is one of our best financial secrets that saved us when I lost my job. We only buy vehicles that are at least three years old, have less than 36,000 miles, and can be paid off within thirty-six months. Why three years? If you buy a brand-new car, as soon as you drive it off the car lot, it will be worth way less than what you paid for it.

Why is this? Well, the dealer bought the car for say, $25,000 from the manufacturer that made the new vehicle. The dealer has to pay rent and electricity, pay the salesman so he can eat, and pay management for all the marketing and great advice. So, the dealer has to sell the car for $30,000 to cover all of these expenses.

If you lose your job after driving the vehicle back and forth to work for one year, how much do you think people will want to buy your car for? It will definitely be less than the $25,000 manufacturer price. So, after three years, the value of a car starts to stabilize because you are no longer paying for the extra overheard that it took to sell the new vehicle with the nice pretty bow on top. So, after three years, you can probably buy that $30,000 car for $20,000.

We want to buy a car with less than 36,000 miles because it has less wear and tear and may even have a few months of warranty left. We will only finance a car for a maximum period of thirty-six months because if one of us was to lose our job for six months, we could quickly sell the car. For example: If we bought a used car that had a sticker price of $12,800 and we paid a down payment of $2,000, we would owe $10,800. If we made twelve payments of $300 a month, we would have a balance of about $7,200 ($12,800 - $5,600). There would be plenty of people who would be willing to buy our car for $7,200. Thus, we would have eliminated $300 in monthly debt if one of us became unemployed due to the company downsizing, a pandemic, or a recession.

Here is how we used to buy our vehicles. So, if our budget was $300 per month, we would find a car that was below $12,800 ($300 x 36 months) + $2,000 down payment. We would search CarMax's website for a car that was three years old, had less than 36,000 miles and was priced under $12,800. We have always gotten great cars from CarMax. They do a great job of providing quality vehicles at an affordable price. Most of the times there would be two or three vehicles that met our criteria and then when we would look at them in person, the color would be off, or the vehicle's features would be outdated.

So, we would drive around from dealership to dealership looking for our diamond in the rough. Most cars being advertised at the small used car lots that met our criteria during our online search would be salvaged vehicles, smelled like a cigarette factory when we inspected them, or had cosmetic damage. We would spend weeks driving around town and checking CarMax's inventory. As usual, during week two or three of our car search, CarMax would have the car that we were looking for.

As we became more financially savvy, we started paying cash for our cars and enjoying having the title of ownership in our names instead of the bank's name. This allowed us to live within our means, save money by not paying extra interest, and most importantly, live freely instead of being tied to a heavy ball of debt.

## Pay Off All Credit Cards And Furniture Loans ASAP

If someone asked you for $5,000 today and told you that in thirty years that they would give you $21,643.83*, guaranteed in writing, would you make the deal? I would! That is a great deal. That is the same deal that the credit card companies are making with you when you charge $5,000 for that shiny new phone, MUST-have, great vacation, or newest wardrobe.

If you charge $5,000 and make the minimum payment for thirty years, you would have paid $21,643.83 for your $5,000 of WANTS. If you cannot afford it, don't buy it. If you have credit cards, pay them off FAST! FAST! FAST! They are robbing you of your retirement.

*To see the impact of paying off a credit card making only the minimum payment, consider a credit card balance of $5,000, at the current average APR of 21.21% (as of January 2020), and minimum payment as 2% of your credit card balance. Making minimum payments only, it would take you over thirty years and $21,643.83 in finance charges to pay off this debt. That doesn't include any fees you might pay over the life of the credit card balance. You are legally being robbed of your retirement if you do this.

## Rule Of 72

The rule of 72 is a quick way to estimate how long it will take for a fixed amount of money to double, depending on the rate at which it earns interest.

It works like this. You have $10,000 and have two options. **Option A** is to deposit the $10,000 into a savings account earning **2%** interest per year and **Option B** is to invest the $10,000 in the stock market, which earns **9%** on average per year. The rule of 72 says to divide the rate of return of the investment by 72 and that is approximately how long it will take to double your money. **Option A** would take the number 72 divide by 2 = 36 years for your $10,000 to double to approximately $20,000. **Option B** would take the number 72 divide by 9 = 8 years for your $10,000 to double to approximately $20,000. The investment selections that you make for your TSP/401K account and your individual retirement account will have a tremendous effect on how early you can retire.

## Get The Free TSP/401K Money

Almost all employers offer a 401K or TSP account to help you retire. If someone told you that if you put $1 in the piggy bank, they would also put $1 into your piggy bank, would you put money in the piggy bank? YES, YES, and YES! Well, that is what your employer is doing when you open up a TSP/401K employee retirement account.

Now, with such a great deal, you are probably thinking, well I will put my entire paycheck of $3,000 for the month into the piggy bank and my employer will also put $3,000 into my piggy bank. However, your employer would go out of business very fast if they did this for all of their employees, so they put a cap on how much money they will put into your piggy bank. Most employers offer a match that ranges from 3% to 5%. So, if you make $40,000 and your employer matches up to 5% that means that if you contribute $2,000 ($40,000 x 5%) into your TSP/401K account, your employer will also put in $2,000. So, at the end of the year, your account will have $4,000 going into it.

Now, like most people, you are probably wondering which funds you should actually invest your money in. I put 50% in the S&P 500 TSP/C Fund and 50% in Small Cap/TSP S Fund in order to get the highest rate of return by investing in the 500 largest US stocks and a basket of US small stocks. If you have $4,000 and 50% goes into the S&P 500 and 50% goes into the Small Cap fund for thirty years, you will have about ($4,000 x 30 years = $120,000) + (Return on your investment $424,224 at 9%) = $545,224.

Total Savings in US Dollars

| Years | Future Value (9.00%) | Total Contributions |
|---|---|---|
| Year 0 | $0.00 | $0.00 |
| Year 1 | $3,999.96 | $3,999.96 |
| Year 2 | $8,359.92 | $7,999.92 |
| Year 3 | $13,112.27 | $11,999.88 |
| Year 4 | $18,292.33 | $15,999.84 |
| Year 5 | $23,938.60 | $19,999.80 |
| Year 6 | $30,093.04 | $23,999.76 |
| Year 7 | $36,801.37 | $27,999.72 |
| Year 8 | $44,113.45 | $31,999.68 |
| Year 9 | $52,083.62 | $35,999.64 |
| Year 10 | $60,771.11 | $39,999.60 |
| Year 11 | $70,240.47 | $43,999.56 |
| Year 12 | $80,562.07 | $47,999.52 |
| Year 13 | $91,812.62 | $51,999.48 |
| Year 14 | $104,075.72 | $55,999.44 |

| Total Savings in US Dollars | | |
|---|---|---|
| Years | Future Value (9.00%) | Total Contributions |
| Year 15 | $117,442.49 | $59,999.40 |
| Year 16 | $132,012.27 | $63,999.36 |
| Year 17 | $147,893.34 | $67,999.32 |
| Year 18 | $165,203.70 | $71,999.28 |
| Year 19 | $184,071.99 | $75,999.24 |
| Year 20 | $204,638.43 | $79,999.20 |
| Year 21 | $227,055.85 | $83,999.16 |
| Year 22 | $251,490.84 | $87,999.12 |
| Year 23 | $278,124.97 | $91,999.08 |
| Year 24 | $307,156.18 | $95,999.04 |
| Year 25 | $338,800.20 | $99,999.00 |
| Year 26 | $373,292.17 | $103,998.96 |
| Year 27 | $410,888.43 | $107,998.92 |
| Year 28 | $451,868.35 | $111,998.88 |

Total Savings in US Dollars

| Years | Future Value (9.00%) | Total Contributions |
|---|---|---|
| Year 29 | $496,536.46 | $115,998.84 |
| Year 30 | $545,224.70 | $119,998.80 |

## Open Up An Individual Retirement Account

Once you get the FREE $$$/Money Match from your employer, it is time to open an Individual Retirement Account (IRA). You can open up a traditional IRA where you put money into your account up to the IRS maximum and the amount is not included in your yearly earnings for tax purposes. The money will grow and then when you reach your minimum retirement age, you must start to make minimum withdrawals, which will be included in your yearly earnings and taxed.

If you open a ROTH IRA and put money into your account up to the IRS maximum, the amount will be included in your yearly earnings for tax purposes, but the earnings will grow tax free*. In addition to the tax benefits of an IRA, you have more investment funds to invest in compared to most employer-sponsored retirement accounts.

Some people choose to invest 100% in the S&P 500 while other people will choose to invest 70% in S&P 500 and 30% in a Bond fund because in the event of a stock market crash, they will not panic and sell all of their stocks at the worst possible time.

A small group of people will choose to invest in an all-around stock portfolio which includes precious metals and real estate that should go up in value despite what is happening in the economy.

If you put $6,000 in your IRA for thirty years, you will have ($6,000 x 30 years = $180,000 + (Return on your investment $637,845 at 9%) = $817,845.

Total Savings in US Dollars

| Years | Future Value (9.00%) | Total Contributions |
|---|---|---|
| Year 0 | $0.00 | $0.00 |
| Year 1 | $6,000.00 | $6,000.00 |
| Year 2 | $12,540.00 | $12,000.00 |
| Year 3 | $19,668.60 | $18,000.00 |
| Year 4 | $27,438.77 | $24,000.00 |
| Year 5 | $35,908.26 | $30,000.00 |
| Year 6 | $45,140.01 | $36,000.00 |
| Year 7 | $55,202.61 | $42,000.00 |
| Year 8 | $66,170.84 | $48,000.00 |
| Year 9 | $78,126.22 | $54,000.00 |
| Year 10 | $91,157.58 | $60,000.00 |
| Year 11 | $105,361.76 | $66,000.00 |
| Year 12 | $120,844.32 | $72,000.00 |
| Year 13 | $137,720.31 | $78,000.00 |

| | | |
|---|---|---|
| Year 14 | $156,115.14 | $84,000.00 |
| Year 15 | $176,165.50 | $90,000.00 |
| Year 16 | $198,020.39 | $96,000.00 |
| Year 17 | $221,842.23 | $102,000.00 |
| Year 18 | $247,808.03 | $108,000.00 |
| Year 19 | $276,110.75 | $114,000.00 |
| Year 20 | $306,960.72 | $120,000.00 |
| Year 21 | $340,587.18 | $126,000.00 |
| Year 22 | $377,240.03 | $132,000.00 |
| Year 23 | $417,191.63 | $138,000.00 |
| Year 24 | $460,738.88 | $144,000.00 |
| Year 25 | $508,205.38 | $150,000.00 |
| Year 26 | $559,943.86 | $156,000.00 |
| Year 27 | $616,338.81 | $162,000.00 |
| Year 28 | $677,809.30 | $168,000.00 |
| Year 29 | $744,812.14 | $174,000.00 |
| Year 30 | $817,845.23 | $180,000.00 |

| | | |
|---|---|---|
| Year 31 | $897,451.30 | $186,000.00 |
| Year 32 | $984,221.92 | $192,000.00 |
| Year 33 | $1,078,801.89 | $198,000.00 |
| Year 34 | $1,181,894.06 | $204,000.00 |
| Year 35 | $1,294,264.53 | $210,000.00 |
| Year 36 | $1,615,125.87 | $216,000.00 |
| Year 37 | $1,772,889.61 | $222,000.00 |
| Year 38 | $1,945,452.67 | $228,000.00 |
| Year 39 | $2,134,203.35 | $234,000.00 |
| Year 40 | $2,340,660.14 | $240,000.00 |

https://www.investor.gov/financial-tools-calculators/calculators/compound-interest-calculator

# How Much Is Your Social Security Worth?

How much is your Social Security Worth?

Like most people, you know that Social Security will not be enough to cover all of your retirement expenses, but exactly how much will the shortfall be for you? In order to determine how much you can expect to receive in Social Security if you retire at your normal retirement age, you will need to do two simple things:

1. Go to the social security site so that you can create your SSN account.

2. Go to page X and you will see your estimated benefit amount at age sixty-seven, with or without spousal survivor benefit. The average employee who makes $40,000 will receive about $18,000, which is 45% of your salary. (This is just an estimate, please contact the social security office about your exact benefits).

Can you afford to retire at age 67?

If you receive $18,000 from Social Security per year, you are almost there. Now, how do you know if the $420,000 in your TSP/401K account and $630,000 in your IRA will be enough to retire with?

For simplicity's sake, most financial planners will say that you can expect to withdraw 4% from your account for thirty years without the account running out of money. If you have $1,050,000 ($420,000 + $630,000) and withdraw 4%, you will have $42,000 each year. So, you will have a yearly post-retirement income of about $60,000 ($18,000 from Social Security and $42,000 from your TSP/401K and IRA account).

# My Accidental Millionaire Retirement Plan

When I became a US Diplomat, a benefit that I did not know about was that I would receive the equivalent of a $2,280,674 Million Dollar retirement package after working for twenty years. This was a BIG blessing! At age fifty-two, I will receive a $50,000 yearly pension which is worth $1,250,000 ($1,250,000 x 4% withdrawal = $50,000) + a Social Security Supplement of $10,000 to age 57 which is worth $250,000 ($250,000 x 4% withdrawal = $10,000).

Then when I turn fifty-nine and a half or per the current IRS rules, I will have access to my TSP account which will be worth at least $780,674 if I put in 5% of my salary to include promotions and step increases in my TSP, and the USG matches my contributions and puts in 5%.

| Year | Contributions[1] | Contribution Growth | Total Projected Balance |
|---|---|---|---|
| 0 | $0.00 | $0.00 | $0.00 |
| 1 | $6,000.02 | $255.78 | $6,255.80 |
| 2 | $12,240.02 | $1,084.80 | $13,324.82 |
| 3 | $18,729.62 | $2,560.66 | $21,290.28 |
| 4 | $25,478.70 | $4,764.46 | $30,243.16 |
| 5 | $32,497.92 | $7,785.55 | $40,283.47 |
| 6 | $39,797.94 | $11,722.20 | $51,520.14 |
| 7 | $47,389.94 | $16,682.65 | $64,072.59 |
| 8 | $55,285.62 | $22,785.76 | $78,071.38 |
| 9 | $63,496.94 | $30,162.21 | $93,659.15 |
| 10 | $72,036.90 | $38,955.50 | $110,992.40 |
| 11 | $80,918.50 | $49,323.38 | $130,241.88 |
| 12 | $90,155.26 | $61,438.89 | $151,594.15 |
| 13 | $99,761.48 | $75,491.81 | $175,253.29 |
| 14 | $109,751.98 | $91,690.43 | $201,442.41 |
| 15 | $120,142.10 | $110,263.11 | $230,405.21 |
| 16 | $130,947.70 | $131,460.14 | $262,407.84 |
| 17 | $142,185.68 | $155,555.86 | $297,741.54 |
| 18 | $153,873.20 | $182,850.75 | $336,723.95 |

| Year | Contributions[1] | Contribution Growth | Total Projected Balance |
|---|---|---|---|
| 19 | $166,028.20 | $213,674.00 | $379,702.20 |
| 20 | $178,669.40 | $248,386.01 | **$427,055.41** |
| 21 | $178,669.40 | $286,821.02 | $465,490.42 |
| 22 | $178,669.40 | $328,715.17 | $507,384.57 |
| 23 | $178,669.40 | $374,379.77 | $553,049.17 |
| 24 | $178,669.40 | $424,154.22 | $602,823.62 |
| 25 | $178,669.40 | $478,408.33 | $657,077.73 |
| 26 | $178,669.40 | $537,545.32 | $716,214.72 |
| 27 | $178,669.40 | $602,004.63 | $780,674.03 |

https://www.tsp.gov/calculators/how-much-will-my-savings-grow/#top

In addition, I will have access to my IRA account at age fifty-nine and a half, or per recent IRS rules, which will be worth about $306,000. I like to use M1 Finance because you can have money withdrawn from your personal bank account every two weeks and deposited into your IRA account. Once the money is deposited into your IRA account, it can be invested automatically in your 100% S&P 500 stock portfolio, 70% stock/30%

bond portfolio or 20% Gold, 20% Bonds, 20% Real Estate, 20% Mid Cap stocks and 20% S&P 500 stock portfolio. You can even invest in dividend growth stocks that pay a dividend every quarter like Coca Cola, if you want. These are only examples of investment options that are available, however, you will need to do your own research or consult a financial advisor.

Total Savings in US Dollars

| Years | Future Value (9.00%) | Total Contributions |
|---|---|---|
| Year 0 | $0.00 | $0.00 |
| Year 1 | $6,000.00 | $6,000.00 |
| Year 2 | $12,540.00 | $12,000.00 |
| Year 3 | $19,668.60 | $18,000.00 |
| Year 4 | $27,438.77 | $24,000.00 |
| Year 5 | $35,908.26 | $30,000.00 |
| Year 6 | $45,140.01 | $36,000.00 |
| Year 7 | $55,202.61 | $42,000.00 |

| | | |
|---|---|---|
| Year 8 | $66,170.84 | $48,000.00 |
| Year 9 | $78,126.22 | $54,000.00 |
| Year 10 | $91,157.58 | $60,000.00 |
| Year 11 | $105,361.76 | $66,000.00 |
| Year 12 | $120,844.32 | $72,000.00 |
| Year 13 | $137,720.31 | $78,000.00 |
| Year 14 | $156,115.14 | $84,000.00 |
| Year 15 | $176,165.50 | $90,000.00 |
| Year 16 | $198,020.39 | $96,000.00 |
| Year 17 | $221,842.23 | $102,000.00 |
| Year 18 | $247,808.03 | $108,000.00 |
| Year 19 | $276,110.75 | $114,000.00 |
| Year 20 | $306,960.72 | $120,000.00 |
| Year 21 | $340,587.18 | $126,000.00 |
| Year 22 | $377,240.03 | $132,000.00 |
| Year 23 | $417,191.63 | $138,000.00 |
| Year 24 | $460,738.88 | $144,000.00 |

| | | |
|---|---|---|
| Year 25 | $508,205.38 | $150,000.00 |
| Year 26 | $559,943.86 | $156,000.00 |
| Year 27 | $616,338.81 | $162,000.00 |
| Year 28 | $677,809.30 | $168,000.00 |
| Year 29 | $744,812.14 | $174,000.00 |
| Year 30 | $817,845.23 | $180,000.00 |
| Year 31 | $897,451.30 | $186,000.00 |
| Year 32 | $984,221.92 | $192,000.00 |
| Year 33 | $1,078,801.89 | $198,000.00 |
| Year 34 | $1,181,894.06 | $204,000.00 |
| Year 35 | $1,294,264.53 | $210,000.00 |
| Year 36 | $1,615,125.87 | $216,000.00 |
| Year 37 | $1,772,889.61 | $222,000.00 |
| Year 38 | $1,945,452.67 | $228,000.00 |
| Year 39 | $2,134,203.35 | $234,000.00 |
| Year 40 | $2,340,660.14 | $240,000.00 |

https://www.investor.gov/financial-tools-calculators/calculators/compound-interest-calculator

# Teach Your Children To Save Money

In addition to my retirement account, I have opened custodial accounts for my children so that they can learn about owning business/stocks at an early age. When they graduate from college and start working, they will automatically buy stocks every pay period so that they can become financially independent to retire at an early age. If they invest $6,000 a year at age twenty-five until age sixty for a total of thirty-five years, they will have about $1.29 million. If they invest $6,000 a year at age twenty-five until age sixty-five for a total of forty years, they will have about $2.34 million.

# Conclusion

In life, I have learned that it is not about where you start, but what it is that you choose to do to stay in the race. You can choose to be upset that you are not at the front of the line when the guns go off or you can choose to do something about it by taking a single step. I am always cognizant that despite the fact that I did not come from a home with wealthy parents, things could have been worse for me. There are those that have started life off so far behind me and yet they too have chosen to run instead of sitting down. I am always inspired by the lives of those that came from nothing and made something for themselves and others.

It is true that there are those who will always have more and do more because they had a great start, but you should not let that control your life. There have been many people who came from riches or made millions, yet they ended up broke because they stopped moving. As long as you never give up and take action by at least crawling if you cannot walk, or walking if you cannot jog, you will be successful.

I hope that this book has inspired you to take some sort of action that you have been putting off for a long time. I look forward to you sharing your results with others.

*Please help a friend by taking one minute of your time to provide a review of the book online wherever you purchased the book.*

*Your action will inspire others to act.*

***Thanks for your support!***

# Author

Michael Dillard was born in Portsmouth, Virginia but was raised for most of his childhood in Clarksville, Tennessee. He graduated from Northeast High School and is a member of the Austin Peay State University Upward Bound Program. As a Foreign Service Officer he has worked in the Dominican Republic, Zambia, Afghanistan, the Democratic Republic of Congo, and South Africa.

In addition, he served four years in the U.S. Army as a radio repairer. He was stationed at Ft. Carson, Colorado; Camp Casey, South Korea, and Ft. Stewart, Georgia.

He received his Bachelors Degree in Interdisciplinary Studies from Middle Tennessee State University, a Master in Business Administration with a concentration in Financial Planning from Strayer University, and a Masters Degree in Accounting from Liberty University.

He completed his ICF executive coach training from the Center for Executive Coaching.

Gain inspiration from Michael Dillard's rise to success and learn how to see obstacles as achievement markers by scheduling a one of kind coaching session with him today!

www.madillard.com

info@madillard.com